tries, the turnpikes are excellent; and that the mountainous roads are, in moſt parts, as good as the nature of the country will admit of; that the inns, with a few exceptions, are comfortable, and that the people are univerſally civil and obliging.

The author has only to regret, that he did not make his tour more complete, for he is now convinced, that he omitted to ſee many places, as well in the principality, as in Monmouthſhire, which would have richly repaid his curioſity. But the little intelligence he could learn from former publications, and the trifling aſſiſtance he could obtain from the natives, muſt plead his excuſe.

As

As the names of the places in the Tour are written according to the Welsh orthography, it is neceſſary to inform the Engliſh reader, that the material difference of pronunciation depends on the following characters.

C, in Welſh, is pronounced as *K* in Engliſh.

F, as *V*.

G, as *G* hard in *Gun*: and never ſoft as in *Gin*.

W, as *Oo* in *Good*.

Dd, as *Th*.

Ll, as *Thl*, ſtrongly aſpirated.

Y, in

Y, in any fyllable of a word, except the laft, as *U* in *burn*: but in
the laft fyllable, as the Englifh *I* in
*Birth.*

A fpecimen of the two laft characters occurs in the word Llanvyllyn, a town in Montgomeryfhire,
which is pronounced *Thlan-vuth-lin.*

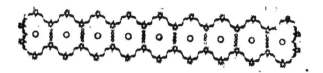

# A
# TOUR
### THROUGH
## MONMOUTHSHIRE and WALES.

THE paffage from Auft to Beach-
ley is about two miles over, and the
road from thence to Chepftow leads
through an agreeable neck of land,
wafhed on each fide either by the Severn or Wye.

B

The

The fhores of the Wye are bold, rocky and woody; but the capital object which catches the eye, on the approach to Chepftow, is the caftle, founded on a high, perpendicular cliff, rifing from the river, and extended along the edge of it.

The whole fortrefs, occupied feveral acres, and the ruins of it are ftill very confiderable. The principal gateway, has a venerable afpect, and though of Norman origin, and the oldeft part of the whole ftructure, is nearly perfect. Several Roman bricks are mixed among the other materials, and in the outward wall

of

of the north fide of the chapel, five or fix courfes of them appear between the facings of the ftone.

This caftle was confidered as very important to both parties, in the civil wars of the laft century; for the authority of the king or parliament prevailed in thefe weftern parts, as either of them was in poffeffion of it. It continued garrifoned even fince the reftoration; and Henry Martin, one of the king's judges, died a prifoner here, after a clofe confinement for many years.

The

The parifh church of Chepftow is part of the old priory, and the weft entrance is a handfome arch of Norman architecture, ornamented with the mouldings peculiar to that people.

Tintern Abbey is fituated on the banks of the Wye, a few miles above Chepftow. No monaftical ruin in Great-Britain prefents a more beautiful perfpective than the infide of the abbey church. The prefent remains are carefully preferved from further deftruction, and the fallen ornaments of its once vaulted roof, are fo difpofed, in moderate piles, that all their fculpture, which is remarkably fharp,

and

and well executed, may be infpected with the utmoft facility.

The body of the church is in its original level, and though the pavement has long fince been removed, I fcarcely lamented the lofs of it, as the fubftituted turf, clean and entirely free from weeds and briars, has perhaps a better effect.

The length of the nave is 230 feet, and the breadth of it 33. The crofs ifle is 160 feet long.

This abbey was founded in the year 1131, but, I fhould imagine, the prefent

fent church was begun feveral years
afterwards, as it is an elegant fpecimen of the chafte Gothic, and conftructed upon one plan and in one
ftyle : the form of the pillars, which
are cluftered in triplets, with light
fhafts a little detached from their
junction, and the turn of the arches,
are not unlike thofe in the cathedral
of Salifbury, which was not founded
till the year 1217, nor finifhed till
1256.

The views from the Wye, between
Chepftow and Tintern, are exceedingly magnificent : the rocks on each
fide feem to be from 300 to 600 feet
high ;

high; they are fometimes perpendicular and wholly naked, and fometimes the very precipices are covered with woods, from the river's brink to their fummits, for continued miles.

On the top of one of thefe mantled mountains, are the well-known gardens of Perffield, which command a large part of this awful profpect.

At Caldecot is the fhell of a caftle, which was built in the Norman age, as the mixture of the circular and Gothic arches fufficiently proves.

Caer-

Caerwent is at prefent a miferable village, and has nothing to manifeft its Roman greatnefs, excepting fome ruined walls on the fouth and weft fides.

The country is here pleafantly inclofed, and near Caerleon the views are extenfive and fine.

Giraldus Cambrenfis gives the following account of this ancient city; and as I fhall have frequent occafion to mention the name of Giraldus, who was my principal guide through the principality, it may not be amifs to premife, that he attended Baldwin,

arch-

archbifhop of Canterbury, in his itinerary through Wales, in the year
1188, who undertook this trouble-
fome and difficult enterprize, not, as
is generally underftood, to convert
the Welfh to Chriftianity, for that re-
ligion was very early eftablifhed in
Wales; but to preach the crufade,
for the recovery of the Holy Land,
which by the diffentions of the Chri-
ftian princes had lately been loft.

I am aware that Giraldus is generally confidered as a mere fabulous
writer; and I grant that he has foiled
every page of his Itinerary with le-
gendary miracles; but, notwithftanding,

ing, I found him a very ufeful and agreeable companion, in his hiftory of the Welfh buildings, and in his defcriptions of that country. But to proceed,

" *Dicitur Caerleon urbs legionum. Caer enim Britannicè* urbs *vel* caftrum *dicitur. Solent quippe legiones à Romanis in infulam tranfmiffæ ibi hyemare, et inde urbs legionum dicta eft. Erat autem hæc urbs antiqua et authentica, et à Romanis olim coatilibus muris egregie conftructa. Videas hic multa priftinæ nobilitatis adhuc veftigia : palatia immenfa aureis olim tectorum faftidiis Romanos faftus imitantia, eo quod* à Ro-

*à Romanis principibus primo conftruc-*
*ta, et ædificiis egregiis, illuftrata fuif-*
*fent : turrim giganteam : thermas in-*
*fignes : templorum reliquias, et loca the-*
*atralia muris egregiis partim adhuc ex-*
*tantibus, omnia claufa.   Reperies ubi-*
*que tam intra murorum ambitum, quam*
*extra, ædificia fubterranea : aquarum*
*duɛtus hypogeofque meatus.   Et quod*
*inter alia notabile cenfui, ftuphas un-*
*dique videas miro artificio confertas,*
*lateralibus quibufdam à præanguftis fpi-*
*raculi viis occulte calorem exhalantibus.*
*Situs urbis egregius fuper Ofcæ flumen,*
*navigio mari influente idoneum.   Syl-*
*vis et parcis urbs illuftrata eft."*

" It

" It is called Caerleon, the city of the legions ; for *caer*, in the British language, fignifies *city* or *caftle* ; and becaufe the Roman legions, which were fent into this ifland, were accuftomed to winter in this place, it acquired the name of Caerleon.   This city is of great antiquity and fame, and was ftrongly defended by the Romans with brick walls.  Many remains of its ancient magnificence are ftill extant ; fuch as fplendid palaces, which once emulated, with their gilded roofs, the grandeur of Rome ; for it was originally built by the emperors, and adorned with ftately edifices : immenfe baths ; ruins of temples,

ples, and a theatre, the walls of which are ftill ftanding. Here we ftill fee, both within and without the walls, fubterraneous buildings, aquieducts, and vaulted caverns; and what appeared to me moft remarkable, ftoves fo excellently contrived, as to diffufe their heat through fecret and imperceivable pores. The city is pleafantly fituated on the banks of the navigable Ufke, and furrounded with woods and pafture."

Great credit is due to this defcription, and I have no doubt, but that it is an accurate reprefentation of the ftate of Caerleon in the twelfth century.

Various

Various antiquities have, in different ages, been difcovered among the
ruins of this city.   Camden and his
continuator have preferved a confiderable catalogue of them ;  and, even
at this time, the fund is not exhaufted.

The Roman walls are ftill vifible,
but the facing ftones have long fince
been removed for private ufes.   Near
the centre of a field, adjoining to the
weft wall,  is the theatre (or more
properly the amphitheatre) mentioned
by Giraldus.

*except on
SW fide in
Mr Morgan's
garden. (Str.)*

The form of it only remains, no
traces of its walls being now difco-
verable:

verable : the diameter of the area is very large, and is bounded with a high circular intrenchment of earth.

There is very little extant of the caftle, which is of a later age ; the keep is remarkably lofty, and on climbing up the fteep fides of it, I blundered upon a curious piece of Roman antiquity.

It was part of a circular ftone, flat on one fide, and convex on the other, 27 inches in diameter : on the flat furface is reprefented in bas relief, a female figure fitting : one hand inclines downwards, and a fmall dolphin

phin is fporting in the palm of the other, which is extended.   There is a broad foliage round the edge of the ftone, which, refembling a myrtle leaf, ferves as a border to it.

On the convex fide are fome circular mouldings, but the centre, which is about ten inches in diameter, is plain and unworked, and probably was originally fixed to a pedeftal.

The figure is indifputably intended for a Venus, and both the defign and execution of it, when perfect, in my opinion, far furpaffed the general fpecimens

cimens of fculpture, which the Romans left in Britain.

This bas relief has been hitherto unknown, and though it was accidentally difcovered, among the ruins, about two years fince, yet fuch was the ignorance of the people, that it it was neglected, and thrown afide, as a ftone of no value, while the meaner materials were found ufeful in mending the roads.

I cannot recollect to have feen Venus ever defcribed with a dolphin in her hand, as in this figure; though Cupid has frequently been thus re-

C　　　　prefented,

prefented, according to the following lines, quoted by Auguftinus, in his explanation of ancient gems :

" *Non fruftra manibus tenet delphinem et florem,*
" *Hic enim terram, ille vero mare habet.*

An exact reprefentation of the prefent ftate of this antiquity, is given in the frontifpiece, drawn on the fpot, and flightly etched by my friend and companion in the tour, to whofe kindnefs alfo the reader is indebted for the notes to this little work.

Many of the Roman bricks, mentioned by Camden, are fcattered about the town ; LEG. II. AVG. is ftrong-

ly

ly imprinted on them, in relievo; and on one I obferved LECLAVG, which might poffibly be intended for the fame characters, though I was ftrong-ly inclined to think the laft meant *Legio Claudii Augufti*.

*LEGI; AVG*

In the houfe of a fhoemaker, we were fhewn a large brick tile, 20 inches in length, and 17 broad : this was certainly ufed in an aqueduct, for the fides of its breadth were raifed about three inches, for the purpofe of carrying the water. This tile was quite perfect, of a bright red colour, and had the latter infcription on it.

C 2                    The

The prefent Caerleon is a melancholy contraft to the ancient, and has fcarcely a decent houfe in it.

Newport is a confiderable town, and was formerly ftrengthened with a fmall caftle, fituated on the river's brink, the fhell of which is ftill pretty entire.

The bridges over the Ufke, both at Newport and Caerleon, and over the Wye at Chepftow, are built upon exceeding high piles of wood: they are floored with boards, which are always loofe, but prevented from flipping by fmall tenons at their ends:

the

the precaution of having the boards unfixed is not unneceffary, as the tides in thefe rivers fometimes rife to a ftupendous height, and would otherwife blow up the bridges.

The roads had hitherto been perfectly good, and though the turnpike is not continued to Caerphily, yet it is a very paffable coach road.

The whole ride is pleafant, at the foot of high hills, generally cultivated to their fummits; and from Machen, the river Rhymny was our guide to Bedways bridge, which carried us into Glamorganfhire.

C 3                    The

The town of Caerphyli confifts of a few ftraggling cottages, and is fur-rounded with mountains, ruder and lefs cultivated than thofe which we had paffed.

The caftle, including the outworks, is of an immenfe fize ; part of the prefent building was conftructed in the year 1221, the ancient caftle hav-ing been razed in 1217.

This part, which is included with-in the inner moat, is a noble ruin ; the hall in it is, excepting the roof, perfect, and is a grand room, being a double cube of 34 feet in breadth ;

the

the form of its Gothic windows, and
of the cluſtered flying pillars between
them, from which ſprang the vaulted
arch of its roof, has a noble appearance.

Gibſon's laboured account of this
room is not conſiſtent with his uſual
accuracy ; for nothing can be more
abſurd, than his idea of beams reſting
on the capitals of the cluſtered pillars,
and of the windows being divided, to
ſerve the purpoſe of enlightening two
chambers.

If this were true, the whole beauty of the hall would effectually be

C 4 loſt ;

loft ; the height of it would be no more than 17 feet, and the elegance of the Gothic windows would only appear on the outfide.

The roof was indifputably vaulted diagonally, and the arches fprang from the pillars, which gave a pro-portionable elevation to the whole.

The hanging tower, in this part of the building, projects about eleven feet beyond its bafe.

The remainder of this caftle has been added, at very different times.

It

It is remarkable, that the eaft wall, on the fouth fide of the principal entrance, is concave, between the large upright buttreffes : thefe buttreffes refemble towers, and had battlements on their tops, to protect the intermediate wall.

The more modern fortifications are extended to a great diftance, and particularly on the north weft fide of the old moat ; for here we fee a high pentagon entrenchment of earth, the angles of which have a circular kind of baftion; and ftill farther north weft, and only divided by another moat, is a large triangular field, moated

round,

round, with a circular mound at each corner.

The veſtiges of a draw-bridge appear on the weſt ſide of the original caſtle, which connected it with
a large piece of high level ground,
embanked round, the walls of which
embankment are ſtill viſible ; and on
the farther ſide of it are the remains
of a round tower.

In all probability, theſe great outworks were added by the younger
Spenſer, who held this caſtle for king
Edward the Second, and who was beſieged in it, by the queen's and the
barons'

barons' forces, in the year 1326. According to Camden, Spenſer defended it ſo manfully that his enemies were ſoon compelled to retire.

There is a good road from Caerphyli to the Pont y Prîdd, or the new bridge, over the Taafe; but as we were to return by part of it to Caerdiff, we took a guide over the mountain of Eglwyſillian, which pariſh ſtands near the top of it. The proſpeſts from the mountain were extenſive, but they ſcarcely compenſated for the badneſs of its deſcent, towards the bridge.

The

The Pont y Prîdd confifts of one arch, from bank to bank, over the rapid Taafe, whofe flooded torrent drives every thing before it that offers refiftance ; as two ftone bridges, in this very fpot, have fatally experienced.

This arch is perhaps the largeft in the whole world; for little credit is to be given to Kircher's defcription of the flying bridge in China : I had the curiofity to meafure it, and had the fatisfaction to find my account nearly agree with a plan I afterwards faw at Caerdiff.

It

It is a fegment of a circle ; the chord of it is 140 feet, and the height of the key ftone, from the fpring of the arch, is 34 feet.

The arch is a fine piece of mafon-ry ; but it is fcandaloufly difgraced with a flight ragged parapet of rough ftones.*

About

* This bridge was undertaken, at the expence of the county, by William Edward, a common mafon, who contracted to infure its ftanding for fix years. He firft built a bridge of three arches, which was carried away by the impetuo-fity of the river. He then conceived the noble idea of raifing a fingle arch over this ungovern-able ftream, which he accordingly completed ; but the crown of the arch being very light and thin, was foon after forced upwards, by the hea-vy preffure of the butments.

But

About half a mile above the bridge is a natural fall of the Taafe: we faw it in a ftill feafon ; but though the fall is not very deep, yet the

But not difcouraged by this repeated ill fuc-cefs, he improved on his fecond plan, and exe-cuted the prefent furprifing arch ; in which he has leffened the weight of the butments, by making three circular tunnels through each, which not only anfwer that purpofe, but give a light-nefs and elegance to the ftructure.

Had the remains of fuch an arch been dif-covered among the ruins of Greece or Rome, what pains would be taken by the learned anti-quarians, to difcover the architect! while honeft William Edward ftill remains unnoticed, among his native mountains.

It might look like injuftice not to mention alfo in this place, the name of Thomas Williams, a mill-wright, of the fame neighbourhood, who framed the wooden centre for this ftupendous arch.

broken

broken rocks in the river, the craggy precipice from which it defcends,
and the fylvan ride towards it, form
a pleafing picture.

Nothing can be more agreeable
than the firft fix or feven miles, from
the Pont y Pridd towards Caerdiff,
The road paffes along the fhady bank
of the raging Taafe ; the country
is finely diverfified with the inequa-
lity of the mountains on each fide
of the torrent ; two of them, finely
cloathed with wood, feem almoft to
clofe together ; between which, under
the fmall ruins of Caftle Coch, we
paffed into the vale of Glamorgan.

Caer-

Caerdiff is a populous but ill-built town, nor is there any thing very pleafing in its environs ; its fituation is on a low flat, near the mouth of the Taafe.

The old walls of Caerdiff are very extenfive, and the ruins of them are ftill confiderable. They were probably built, as well as the large octagon tower, on the keep of the caftle, by the firft Norman invaders.

The moft remarkable occurrence in the hiftory of Caerdiff caftle, is, that Robert, eldeft fon of William the Conqueror, and the right heir of

his

his father, to both England and Nor-
mandy, was, after undergoing various viciffitudes of fortune, at length
confined in it by king Henry the
Firft, and here he languifhed, deprived of his fight, for the term of
twenty fix years, when death re-
leafed him from the unnatural cruel-
ties of his brother.

Llandaff ftands on a gentle elevation, but is in reality a paltry village, though a bifhoprick.

The remains of the old cathedral
are very beautiful; the door cafes are
all of Norman work, and well exe-

D                          cuted;

cuted; the reft of it is an elegant Gothic, though it was conftructed fo early as the year 1120, and is perhaps one of the oldeft fpecimens of Gothic in the whole ifland.

The modern cathedral, on which large fums have lately been lavifhed, is a medley of abfurdities: part of the ancient nave is included in it, but the rebuilder has added Roman architecture, mixed with a capricious kind of his own, to the folemnity of the Norman and Gothic *.

In

* In this cathedral are feveral ancient monuments, and among others, two of the anceftors of the Matthews's family, in finely polifhed marble, which have

In order to make the ridicule complete; the Chriſtian altar is raiſed under the portico of a Heathen temple,
which projects into the choir.

The ruins of ſeveral caſtles appear
in the neighbourhood of Cowbridge,
and I am ſorry I did not make an
excurſion to St. Donat's, which, I have

ſince

have uncommon merit, for the age in which they
were done. The head-dreſs and hair of a female
figure, the necklace of different ſtrings, hanging
on her boſom, and other minute parts, are touched
with a delicacy of execution, which would do honour to a modern artiſt. It appears, from Mr.
Walpole's anecdotes, and in the life of Benvenuto
Cellini, that in the reign of that ſumptuous tyrant,
Henry the Eighth, ſeveral Italian ſculptors were
encouraged and employed in England; theſe monuments were probably executed by ſome of them:
a conjecture which the dreſs of the figures ſeems to
confirm.

since been informed, deserved attention.

Cowbridge consists of one broad and
handsome street; it was in this town
that we first met with the fish called
Sewen, which seems to be of the
salmon species, but the flavour, in
my opinion, is much superior. It re-
minded me more of the Berwick
trout, which is so much esteemed in
London.

The southern and western coasts of
Wales, abound with this delicious
fish, in such plenty, that it is frequently sold for three half-pence or
two-pence

two-pence a pound. It was almoſt
a conſtant diſh at our table.

Journeying towards Pile, we left
Wennye caſtle on our right hand,
and Ogmore on our left, both within view of the turnpike.

From our cleanly little inn at Pile,
we made a walking excurſion, in
ſearch of the remains of Cynfeg caſtle, which are more than two miles
diſtant from it.

Scarcely a wall of this caſtle is
now to be ſeen, and the face of the
country muſt have ſuffered great re-
volutions,

D 3

volutions, from the winds and inun-
dations, since Fitzhamon, the first
Norman invader, chose to fix his re-
sidence on this spot.

This fortress was built on one fingle mount, about the size of a common keep, and there do not appear
any vestiges of other fortifications
near it. It is now surrounded with
naked sands, blown up in irregular
heaps, and subject to alterations by
every storm. The present situation
gives no idea of its having been proper, either for pleasure, or defence.

Following the little brook from
the ruins towards our inn, we were
agreeably

agreeably furprized with a remarkable fpring of water, rifing like a
fpout from a fmall pool, which ad-
joins to, and mixes with, the rivulet: it bubbled fo violently, that the
water gufhed upwards more than a
foot above the level of the pool, and
in a fountain as large as a man's
body.

Near Margam, in a lane leading
from thence towards Cynfeg, we faw
one of the ftones noticed by Camden;
it is now placed upright, and the
chara&ters of the fepulchre are ftill
perfe&ly legible, *Punpeius car au-
topius.*

D 4 The

The fituation of Margam abbey,

*Robert*

*James 73)* founded by William earl of Glou-
cefter, grandfon to Fitzhamon, is at
the foot of a high mountain, wholly
covered with wood. I omitted to
fee the orange trees, in the garden
groove, which I have fince heard are
the fineft in all Britain.

In the ftreet of Margam is an ancient crofs, which, with its pedeftal,
is covered with a profufion of fculpture, reprefenting knots and fret-
work. A few characters are feen near
the two figures on it, but I was not
able to decypher them.

The

The abbey church is a Norman edifice, in the beft tafte : the circular arches of the nave are finely proportioned, and the capitals of the. fmall pillars at the weft-door, are more pleafing in their variations than any I have feen : it is ftill ufed as the parifh church, though many parts have greatly fuffered from the injuries of time and violence.

The road is now continued under the mountains, near the Severn fhore, and paffes clofe to fome large copperworks to Aberavon, where it croffes a ftone bridge of one arch, built by the mafon of Pont y Prîdd, and leads

to

to Briton ferry, which croffing, we
rode along the beach for a few miles,
and were ferried over the Tavey into
Swanfea.

The landfcape about Briton ferry
is exceedingly rich : the mountains,
the river, and its woody banks, form
a beautiful back-ground and contraft
to the bold and craggy fhore, and
the broken infulated Knoles near it.

Juft above the ferry is the feat of
Mr. Vernon, fituated in the centre
of this enchanting view.

The

The fea breezes from the Briftol channel have no influence over the verdure of the trees on this fouthern coaft, which flourifh as well here as in the more inland parts.

Swanfea makes a handfome appearance from the approach to it, being built near the mouth of the Tavey, on a femicircular rifing bank above it. The town is populous, and the ftreets are wide; it carries on a confiderable trade in coals, pottery and copper. A large copper-work is conftantly fmoaking within view of the town; and another, ftill larger, employs many hands, a few miles higher up the river, near Neath.

The

The plenty of coal in this neighbourhood, and the convenience of
exportation, have induced the copper
companies to prefer this ſpot to all
others.

Such is the profuſion of coal and
lime ſtone in Glamorganſhire, that
lime is the general manure of the
whole country; and there are few
eſtates, either here or in Monmouthſhire, without the advantage of lime-
pits for that purpoſe. The houſes,
walls, and out-buildings are commonly white-waſhed: and there is
ſcarcely a cottage to be ſeen, which is
not regularly bruſhed over every week.

The

The remaining walls of Swanfea caftle, are finifhed with an open, Gothic parapet, through the arches of which the water ran from the tiles: this was an excellent fecurity to the roofs, as they could be in no danger of being damaged by the fnow, or water being pent up, or confined. This fingular parapet gave a lightnefs and elegance to the building ‡.

Leaving Swanfea, we croffed over the tedious and dreary mountain of

Bettûs,

‡ The approach to this town, would be rendered much more agreeable and convenient, by a bridge acrofs the Tavy, and from the fteepnefs of the banks of this river, if fuch a bridge was to confift of a fingle arch, like the Pont y Pridd, veffels might pafs and repafs under it with all their fails ftanding.

Bettūs, in the midway towards the Llandīlo vawr, (from the extremities of which there is a rich and exténſive proſpect) and deſcended into Caermarthenſhire.

Llandīlo vawr is a ſmall town, hanging on the declivity of a hill waſhed by the Towy.

According to the hiſtory of Wales, by Carādoc of Lhancarvan, the laſt deciſive battle, between the armies of Edward the Firſt and Llewellin, prince of Wales, was fought near this town, when the King's forces gained a complete victory; in conſe-
quence

quence of which, the unfortunate prince, foon after, near Builth, loft both his power and life.

This victory put a final period to the Welch independency, in the year 1282, fince which time the principality has continued fubject to the crown of England.

And furely, this fubjection is efteemed a moft happy circumftance, by every reafonable Briton. The ancient hiftory of Wales is a calendar of ufurpations, depredations, and murders. In a public caufe the principality was frequently united, but,

if

if at any time an interval of peace
fucceeded, with their powerful neighbours, it was conftantly followed by
the moft cruel civil and domeftic
broils; for the government defcend-
ing, like the common eftates, by ga-
velkind, many competitors pretended
to a fhare in it. An equality of
power could not long exift; and no
fooner was the country free from foreign danger, than it became ftained
with the moft unnatural barbarities
and affaffinations. The fword was the
only law. There was neither fafety
to the prince, nor fecurity to the
fubject. The whole country became
a fcene of the moft woeful anarchy,

and

and every one lived in a perpetual jealoufy, and reciprocal dread of each other. This was the ftate of independent Wales, which was more harraffed and weakened by thefe inteftine commotions, than by all the bloody Englifh wars; for indeed, the happieft times which the miferable Britons enjoyed, were thofe in which they were united againft a foreign enemy.

The ruins of Dinevawr Caftle ftand on the high prominence of a beautiful femicircular hill, entirely mantled with wood, and which, with a regular fweep, precipitately defcends to the Towy.

E        We

We learn from Lhwyd's breviary, that Rhys ap Theodore, prince of South Wales, in the time of William the Conqueror, built a caftle on this Spot. He was compelled, by reafon that the fea coafts were continually molefted by the Normans, Englifh, and Flemings, to remove hither from Caermarthen, which had been the royal feat of the princes of Demetia, or South Wales, from the time of the deftruction of Caerleon by the Saxons. Dinevawr, from this time, became the refidence of the Southwallian princes, and the fituation was not unworthy of fuch diftinction.

Giraldus

Giraldus thus fpeaks of it : " *Ca-*
*ftrum Dinevor in collis excelfi vertice*
*fuper fluvium Towy fitum eft : quod et*
*principalis Sudwalliæ* Curia *dicitur.*"

The caftle, which Giraldus faw,
was rafed to the ground in the year
1194, fix years after his itinerary ;
but it was foon rebuilt.

From the extent of the prefent ruins,
I cannot conceive it to have been fo
much a caftle of ftrength and grandeur, as a fmall palace, calculated for
the more refined and focial plea-
fures.

The ruins are now inclofed in the beautiful park of Newton, belonging to Mr. Rice, and adjoining the town of Llandilo.

The caftle of Caraig-cennin ftands four miles S. E. from Llandilo, towards the black mountain : It is moft ftrongly fituated, on the point of a lofty, craggy, infulated rock, three fides of which are wholly inacceffible : it is furrounded, at moderate but unequal diftances, with mountains ; and the roads leading to it are, even now, but barely practicable. The fortrefs, of which there are great remains, does not occupy an acre of ground,

ground, for indeed the rock would not admit of more.

This was doubtlefs a Britifh build-ing; the remaining ruins confirm the fuppofition, as there is not the leaft appearance of Gothic about them.

Might not this impregnable rock have been the citadel of the Britifh princes? and might not Dinevawr, from which it is not more than five miles diftant, be their palace or *Curia*, according to Giraldus?

I could learn nothing in the coun-try, about the derivation of *Cennin*;

E 3 there

there is no river of that name\*. I firſt thought of the Saxon *Konnen*, as it would then ſignify King's Caſtle; but that people never extended their power ſo far in Wales. *Cennin* may be the participle of the Britiſh *Canu*, and it might properly be called the ſinging rock, from its expoſition to the winds.

The well in this caſtle is a ſingular curioſity; for, inſtead of a perpendicular deſcent, which might have

---

\* "I lernid ons that Kennenn Riveret riſith in blake mountaine, and goith into Tewi, about Dinever." Leland's Itin. vol. 5. fol. 23. But I could hear of no ſuch river, nor could I diſcover any traces of it in any of the oldeſt maps.

been

been made with much lefs trouble, we find a large, winding cave, bored through the folid rock.

An arched paffage, on the brink of the precipice, leads along the out-fide of the caftle, with an eafy flope, to the beginning of the perforation, which is in length 84 feet.

The perforation is of various di-menfions; the breadth of it, at the beginning, is 12 feet, and in fome places it is lefs than three, but at a medium, may be eftimated to be from five to fix feet. In fome parts, the cave is ten feet high; in others, not

E 4　　　　more

more than four. The whole length of the defcent through the rock is 150 feet, but the declivity is unequal, fometimes greater, and fometimes lefs; but on an average, it may make an angle of about 30 degrees with the plane of the horizon.

Notwithftanding all this extravagant labour, there is fcarcely water fufficient for a fmall family, nor does there appear, at prefent, any other refources within the precincts of the caftle.

About eight or ten feet from the extremity of the cave, and four feet above

above the ground, there is a fmall
bafon in the rock, which may contain fomething more than a gallon,
into which a little water is continually dropping, in greater or lefs quantities, according to the feafon of the
year, or the ftate of the atmo-
fphere.

This could never anfwer the purpofes of the garrifon, and therefore
we may conclude, as the perforation
is continued beyond the bafon, that
the fcheme was either intended to have
been purfued, or that it was dropped,
through defpair of fuccefs.

A poor

A poor woman in this neighbour-hood told me, fhe had difcovered, about a year fince, with her plough, 150 angular pieces of filver, at the foot of the precipice, and that fhe had given them to her landlord, Mr. Vaughan, of Golden Grove, near Llandilo.

Mr. Vaughan was not in the coun-try, and though I made a diligent enquiry after thefe coins, as thinking they might lead towards the hiftory of the caftle, I could learn no cer-tain particulars about them.

But, fince my return, I have been informed, by a gentleman of Llandilo, who

who was fo obliging as to fend me
moft of the particulars concerning
the well, that the coins had been mif-
reprefented to me, and that they
were of the times of Elizabeth and
Charles the Firft, and confequently,
the common veftiges only of the civil diffentions in the laft century.

Notwithftanding what I have faid
of this extraordinary caftle, I am
aware, that there is no mention made
of it in the hiftory of Caradoc of
Lhancarvan, till the year 1248;
when Rhys Fychan won it from the
Englifh, to whom his mother had
fome time before privately delivered it.
                                    This

This filence about Caraig-cennin appears at firſt remarkable, as the neighbouring caſtles of Llangadock and Llandovery are repeatedly noticed: but as the hiſtorian rarely ſpeaks of the foundation of a caſtle, and ſcarcely ever mentions one, excepting it is beſieged or taken, this caſtle, from its uncommon ſtrength of ſituation, might not fall within the plan of his hiſtory, till the year 1248.

We now continued our rout through a charming country, perfectly cultivated on each ſide of the turnpike.

We

We had a view, on our left hand, of the ruins of ~~Durflon~~ caftle, fituated *Dinslau* on a large natural knole, near the Towy : and foon after paffed through Abergwilly, where is a feat of the Bifhop of St. David's, but which has nothing to recommend it, except the beauty of the neighbouring country.

The fifhermen, in this part of Caermarthenfhire, ufe a fingular kind of boats, called Corăcles.

They are generally five feet and a a half long, and four broad; their bottom is a little rounded, and their fhape is exactly oval. Thefe boats

are

are ribbed with light laths, or split twigs, in the manner of basket-work, and are covered with a raw hide, or strong canvas, pitched in such a manner as to prevent leaking. A seat crosses just above the center, towards the broad end. The men paddle them with one hand and fish with the other, and when their work is finished, bring their boats home with them on their backs.

In riding through Abergwilly, we saw several of these phænomena in the street, with their bottoms upwards, which at first sight appeared

like

like the fhells of fo many enormous
turtles.

Thefe boats are fpecimens of the
original Britifh navigation, according
to Cæfar, who made them turn to a
good account in his Spanifh expedi-
tion againft Pompey; for Cæfar's
bridges over the Segre, being hurried
away by the torrent, he tranfported
his legions acrofs it in veffels of this
conftruction.

" *Imperat militibus Cæfar, ut na-
ves faciant cujus generis eum fuperi-
oribus annis ufus Britanniæ docuerat.
Carinæ primum ac ftatumina ex levi
materiâ*

*materiá fiebant : reliquum corpus na-*
*vium viminibus contextum coriis inte-*
*gebatur."*                Bell. civ. lib. i.


Pliny,  in his account of Britain,
fpeaks of a fix days navigation in the
open fea with thefe coracles.   " *Ti-*
*mæus hiftoricus a Britannia introrfus,*
*fex dierum navigatione abeffe dicit In-*
*fulam Mictim in qua candidum plum-*
*bum proveniat.   Ad eam Britannos*
*vitilibus navigiis corio circumfutis na-*
*vigare.*

Plin. Hift. nat. l. iv. c. 16.


Caermarthen is a large and handfome Welfh town :  I fpeak by comparifon ;

parifon; for, in general, the Welfh ftreets are narrow and winding, and the decent houfes are too often intermixed with the meaneft cottages.

Part of the eaftle is now ufed as the county gaol; but there is nothing remarkable in the ruins of it.

According to Giraldus, the walls of Caermarthen were raifed with brick, but I could not difcover the fmalleft traces in the remains of them; though the rednefs of the ftones at firft deceived me, and inclined me to be of his opinion.

F                    He

He takes no notice of the caftle, and perhaps there was none in his time, though it is generally fuppofed to have been founded in 1110.

A long ftone bridge croffes the Towy from this town ; but, like the common fafhion of the country, it is inconveniently narrow.

The beauty of the country now diminifhes, and there is little worth attention in the road, till we arrive at Narbeth, a fmall town, with fome remains of a caftle in Pembrokefhire. We had indeed a diftant view, on our right hand, of the remarkable mountain

-tain called the Ragged Rocks, the
summit of which appeared circular,
and like the stupendous ruins of a
castle wall.

About two miles forward we crossed the Cleddy, near which, on the
right hand, appear the the remains of
Lauhaden castle, and on the left the
fine woods of Slebach.

It is peculiar to Picton castle, that
it has always been inhabited. The
present possessors are the Philips's, by
whom it has been modernized. It is
esteemed one of the capital houses
in the principality; but the strongest

F 2                    curiosity

curiofity to examine modern architecture, will caufe little interruption
to a.tour through Wales.

Haverfordweft, is a large irregular
town, built on the declivity of a
hill, which is fo fteep towards the
river, that the back windows of the
ground floors in one ftreet, frequently overlook the roofs of another.

The caftle ruins are confiderable,
and prefent a grand object to the
approach from Narbeth.

As we were foon to traverfe a poor
and miferable country, we though it
prudent

prudent to exchange a bank note at Haverfordweft, to prevent the difficulties which might otherwife attend our paffing it : but even here we were delayed feveral hours before we could get money for it : at length ten pounds were raifed and offered for the note, provided I would *endorfe* it.

Methodifm has extended its baneful influence even to this remote angle of our ifland; for two chapels of the different perfuafions of Wefley and Lady Huntingdon, flourifh at Haverfordweft ; they feem to be dedicated to their tutelar faints, for they are only diftinguifhed by the

F 3  names

names of their patrons. Both chapels are regularly crowded ; but whether fuperftition, novelty, or curiofity is the caufe, I fhall not pretend
to determine. I am unwilling to
attribute it to the neglect of the pa-
ftors of the eftablifhed church, nor
can I give credit to that vulgar re-
port.

I have fince feen, in the moft retired fpots of this country, a wretched
cottage nearly burfting with the fullnefs of its congregation ; and multi-
tudes, in a heavy rain, fwarming about
the outfide, imbibing, with gaping
mouths, the poifonous tenets of a
mechanical preacher, which

———creep-

——————————— creeping on,
Spread, like a low-born mist, and blot the fun.

We made an excursion from Haverfordwest to Harbarston Haikin, situated on the broadest part of Milford Haven.

The little harbour of Harbarston is generally full of vessels, which export from it, corn, coals, and limestone; and we found no difficulty in hiring a convenient boat to carry us to Pembroke.

We sailed acrofs the haven of Milford, so well known for its magnitude and security. It appears like

F 4                          an

an immenfe lake, for the mouth not being at any diftance vifible, the whole haven feems land-locked ; the mouth opens to the fouthward, and the haven extends itfelf eaftward.*

* As the fortifying this harbour, and erecting an arfenal, docks, &c. is a fubject that has been much canvaffed of late years, and indeed a fcheme of that kind has been attempted to be carried into execution, at a confiderable national expence ; it may not be amifs to obferve, that although Milford Haven is one of the fineft harbours in Europe, large enough to contain the whole navy of Great Britain, quite fecure againft all winds, with good anchoring ground in every part ; yet the entrance, which is a mile and three quarters broad, is much too wide to be properly defended againft an enemy ; was that even practicable, perhaps the fcarcity of timber in its neighbourhood, would be a powerful objection againft making it a naval feaport.

There

There is nothing bold or picturefque on the fhores of it; they are neither mountainous, nor woody; the land round the haven confifts of fmall inequalities of ground, pretty well cultivated, though fometimes varied with large furze brakes.

The view of Pembroke and its caftle, from the river, is very grand. The town is fituated upon the ridge of a long and narrow rock, gradually afcending to the higheft point, on which ftands the caftle, at the edge of the precipice. If I may compare fmall things with great, it refembles much the fituation of Edinburgh.

The

· The caftle is a Norman ftructure, mixed with the early Gothic : the principal tower, which is uncommonly high and perfect, has even its ftone vaulted roof remaining.

This fortrefs was built by Girald, Conftable of Windfor, anceftor of Cambrenfis, who thus fpeaks of its prior fortification :

" *Primus hoc caftrum Pembrochiæ Arnulphus de Montgomery, fub Anglorum rege Henrico primo, ex virgis et cefpite tenui, fatis exile contruxit.*"

" Arnul-

" Arnulphus of Montgomery originally founded a caftle at Pembroke,
in the reign of Henry I. but it was
a flight rampart, only raifed with
*ofiers* and *turf.*" I neglected to fee
Carew Caftle and Tenby in this
neighbourhood, which, from defcriptions I have fince heard of them,
I greatly regret.

We returned with the tide to Har-
barfton, and 'by the fame road to
our quarters at Haverfordweft, thro'
an inclofed but unpleafant country,
near the little parifh of Harold-
fton, which may poffibly have

taken

taken its name from King Ha-
rold.

There is a particularity in the
dress of the Pembrokeshire women,
which, because it differs from the rest
of the Welsh, I shall describe.

The women, even in the midst of
summer, generally wear a heavy
cloth gown; and instead of a cap, a
large handkerchief wrapt over their
heads, and tied under their chins.

On first seeing this fantastic head
dress, I really imagined that there
was

was an epidemical fwelling or tooth-
ache in the country.

It is poffible that this fafhion might
originate from Flanders, as Pembrokefhire was formerly fettled by
Flemings. In that low country,
this head drefs might have been
thought a neceffary prefervation
againft the damps, and a national
prejudice may have continued it in
Wales, for more than fix centu-
ries.

This cuftom is certainly peculiar
to Pembrokefhire; for in the other
parts of Wales, the women, as well

as

as the men, wear large beaver hats, with broad brims, flapping over their shoulders.

Nay, even some of the better sort of people affect this covering; for I afterwards met, at Llandrindod wells, three old ladies of the neighbourhood, who supped with us, under the shade of their beavered umbrellas. The general prevalence of this latter custom recalled to my memory the fabulous history of Giraldus, concerning beavers being found on the Tywy banks, in Cardiganshire, and might induce a stranger to give some kind of credit to the legend.

From

From Haverfordweſt the road leads through a miſerable country, leaving a ruined tower of Roche caſtle on the right hand, and winds down to the beach of Niwegal, about the midway towards St. David's: it then traverſes a mountain, and deſcends to the romantic little harbour of Solvath, which is a cove, ſurrounded with high and barren rocks.

Giraldus relates a curious circumſtance, which happened to the beach of Niwegal, about ſixteen years before his itinerary, in the following words:

" *Per*

" *Per fabulum de Niwegal tranfi-*
*vimus, ubi et ea tempeftate qua Anglo-*
*rum rex Henricus fecundus in Hiber-*
*niæ finibus hyemavit, nec non et aliis*
*fere cunctis partium illarum portu-*
*bus ab occidente marinis, res contigit*
*non indigna memoratu. Ex nimia ni-*
*mirum præter folitum procellæ vehe-*
*mentia, fabulofis Auftralis Cambriæ*
*littoribus folo tenus fabulo nudatis, lon-*
*gis operta retro feculis, terræ facies*
*apparuit, arborum in ipfum mare fti-*
*pites ftantium undique præcifarum, ic-*
*tufque fecurium tanquam hefterni, ter-*
*ra quoque nigerrima, lignaque trun-*
*corum hebeno fimillima."*

" We

" We then traverfed the fands of
Niwegal, where (at the time that
Henry the Second was compelled, on
account of the ftorms, to winter in
Ireland) and in many other ports of
the weftern fhores, occurred an extraordinary phænomenon ; for, a very violent tempeft drove the fands
from the beach, and expofed land to
view, which had been covered for
many ages.

" Here were now feen, trunks of
trees ftanding in the fea, with the
marks of the axe as vifible on them,
as if they had been lately felled : the
earth was extremely black, and the

G

wood

wood of the trunks refembled ebony, both in colour and hardnefs."

I have been the more particular in citing this extract, becaufe I have heard, from good authority, that the fame circumftance, though in a lefs degree, has been fometimes obferved in modern times. The whole country is now fo barren of wood, that fcarcely a tree is to be feen within fome miles of Niwegal.

A ftreet of wretched cottages, one of which is the inn, compofes the city of St. David's. I had fo little notion of its being the bifhoprick, that

that I enquired in the ftreet, how far it was to St. David's. The reader will eafily give me credit, when he hears that the palace and cathedral ftand below the town, and cannot be feen from it.

The bifhop's palace, which was founded in the reign of Edward the Third, is now an immenfe ruin; feveral of the apartments are uncommonly large, the walls of which are ftill entire. The whole parapet is Gothic, and open in arches like that at Swanfea, a circumftance peculiar to thefe two remains of antiquity.

The

The nave of the cathedral was built in the reign of king John; the circular arches of it are remarkably wide: but the other parts of the church have been the production of different ages, as the variety of architecture plainly demonſtrates. Biſhop Vaughan's chapel was annexed to it in the time of Henry the Eighth, and has a light elegant roof of ſtone, quite perfect. There are ſeveral ancient monuments, both within the church, and among the ruined chapels without. Edmund, earl of Richmond, father of Henry the Seventh, lies under a raiſed tomb, near the middle of the choir, and at a little

diſtance

diftance from it, is the monument of
Owen Tudor.

The choral fervice is performed in
this cathedral, twice a day, but is feldom attended with any congregation.
The whole church is in a very dirty
and flovenly condition ; part of it is
not paved, and the graves are raifed
within it, in the fame manner as in
common churchyards *.

There is fomething fimple and
pleafing, in the idea of ftrewing flo-

* There is probably fome little fee due to the
church, for burying within the walls of the cathedral, which is readily paid by the Cambrians, for
the honour of laying their bones under the fame
roof with Owen Tudor.

wers

wers and ever-greens over the grave of
a departed friend, which is the uni-
verfal cuftom in thefe parts.

> With faireft flow'rs, whilft fummer lafts,
> I'll fweeten thy fad grave.  Thou fhalt not lack
> The flow'r that's like thy face, pale primrofe; nor
> The azur'd hare-bell, like thy veins; no, nor
> The leaf of Eglantine; which not to flander,
> Outfweeten'd not thy breath.
>
> SHAKESPEARE's CYMBELINE.

But when we faw the faded plants,
rotting on the new raifed earth, within the walls of the church, it became
offenfive and difgufting.

I cannot better exprefs the dreari-
nefs of this country, than in the
words of Giraldus, who lies buried

at

at St. David's; but poor Cambrenſis was unknown to the officiating vi-cars, and conſequently his tomb.

" *Hic etenim angulus eſt ſupra Hi-bernicum mare remotiſſimus, terra, ſaxo-ſa, ſterilis et infæcunda: nec ſylvis veſtita, nec fluminibus diſtincta, nec pratis ornata: ventis ſolum et procel-lis ſemper expoſita.*"

" The land about this remote an-gle on the Iriſh ſea, is rocky, barren, and fruitleſs; it is neither cloathed with wood, varied with rivers, nor beautified with meadows, but con-ſtantly expoſed to ſtorms and tempeſts."

G 4                    This

This melancholy defcription is a juft picture of the whole face of the country, with a few exceptions only, for more than eighty miles.

The weftern coaft of Wales is mountainous, with fteep or perpendicular cliffs towards the Irifh fea. In croffing the few rivers in this dreary part of our rout, we had a fharp defcent from one mountain, and a quick afcent to another. The road is commonly within view of the fea, and fometimes of the Irifh coaft.

Few inclofures are to be feen in the neighbourhood of St. David's, and

and the property is regulated in a manner different from that of the open fields in England: for here is no common feed, and every proprietor has a private right to the pasture of his own ground only, and to no other.

This circumstance is attended with much inconvenience, both to the owners of the lands and to the traveller. For, there being no common shepherd, all the horses, sheep, and even poultry, are staked at the end of a line to the ground, in order to prevent mutual trespasses. The confe-

quence

quence of this is, that the ropes frequently crofs the high road, and en-
tangle the horfes feet of the unwary
rider.

I made a fhort excurfion from St.
David's, to fee *y maen figl,* or the
fhaking ftone, mentioned by Gibfon:
it lies near the moft wefterly point of
St. David's head. Its fhaking was certainly a *lufus naturæ*, as it is a frag-
ment fallen from the upper rock,

This ftone has long fince been im-
moveable, but never could be fo curious as the famous rocking ftone, at
Stonehenge in Wiltfhire.

That

That alfo was occafioned by an accident, for the ftone was one of the great impofts of a Trilithon, the mortoifes being ftill vifible at each end of it: one of its pillars was, by fome means or other, forced out of its upright pofition, and the impoft confequently falling, pitched firft on one end, and then fell back on the altar, on which it remains perfect and unbroken, and in fuch exact equilibrium, that it may ftill be put in motion with a fingle hand.

The weight of the two ftones in queftion, appeared to me to be nearly equal.

Fifgard

Fifgard ftands upon the point of a mountain, from which there is a fteep defcent, (cut from the precipice) to its little harbour, at the mouth of the Gwyne.

Within two miles of Newport, a beggarly town, fituated under the ruins of a fmall caftle, the road paffes clofe to the remains of four or five Druid fepulchres, or altars ; the ftones are large, and were originally fupported with four upright pillars, like the legs of a table : they are all within the circumference of about fixty yards, and one of them is nearly perfect.

Thefe

Thefe monuments lie on the left hand of the road, in an inclofed field, which, in Englifh pronunciation, is called Daertinman.

In a fmall field, between Newport and its harbour, is another monument, ftill larger, and quite perfect, of the fame kind; the upper ftone is fhaped like a mufhroom, and is upwards of nine feet in diameter‡.

‡ The landlord of the hovel were we baited, at Newport, on conducting us to thefe ftones, afked our opinion concerning them; and, on our telling him, we conjectured them to be the fepulchral monument of fome *great man* among the ancient Britons, he anfwered, with much fatisfaction, that he entirely agreed with us, and doubted not, but upon digging, the fkeleton of a huge giant would be difcovered.

There

There are many others fimilar in this neighbourhood; but by a mifin-formation, which is too common in Wales, we were directed beyond them, and the day was too far fpent for us to return to fee them.

We found the accommodations fo villanous at Fifgard and Newport, that we thought it prudent to conti-nue our ftage to Cardigan.

The old crofs, mentioned by Gib-fon, remains in the churchyard at Nevern; but we could not find ei-ther the infcribed ftone, on the north fide of the churchyard, or the in-fcription

fcription in the church; nor could we learn any intelligence of them.

The church at Nevern has no pavement in it, and the frequent burials, in the manner of St. David's, have raifed the ground within, feven or eight feet higher than it is without.

This parifh is pleafantly fituated, on the banks of the river Nevern, and backed by fome fine fhady hills: we afcended one of them, and, by a bad and intricate road, arrived at Cardigan, having paffed through the dirty village of St. Dogmael, formerly famous

mous for its abbey, fome ruins of which ftill remain, and which the river Tyvy divides from Cardigan-fhire.

Moft of the ancient monuments in thefe parts, have lately been de-ftroyed, and converted to private ufes; for, though the whole country is a quarry, it is generally of flate, and therefore of no advantage in build-ing.

Cardigan ftands upon a gentle emi-nence, rifing from the Tyvy, over which there is a handfome ftone bridge. Part of the outward walls

of

of the caftle is ftill remaining, but, the materials within, have long fince been removed.

We rode from hence to Llangoidmore, and fending our horfes from thence, round to Llechryd bridge, followed a beautiful fhady path, cut from the precipice of the Tyvy bank, for two miles. This river runs in a broad and tranflucid ftream, between the floping hills, which are about 200 feet in height, and wholly covered with wood, from the water's brink to their fummits. This fylvan fcene is only once interrupted by a lofty, naked, and projecting rock, on which

H ftand

stand the romantic ruins of Cilgarran Castle, and which, by its singular contrast to the rest of the view,
gives a finishing to a delicious land-
scape.*

Cilgarran was originally fortified
by Roger Montgomery, who, with

* The variegated walk, by the side of this river,
and, indeed, the whole scene, bears a strong resem-
blance to the situation of the celebrated Persfield :
and, though the stream below is not so wide, nor
the rocks on each side so awfully grand, yet, the
beautiful verdure of the one, and the transparent
clearness of the other, make ample amends; to
which, if we add the magnificent ruin of Cilgarran
castle, I think Llangoidmore will lose little on the
comparison. Was I indeed to speak from my own
feelings, I should give this spot the preference, on
the whole, to any we saw in Wales, and more particularly so, as very little has been done to orna-
ment or improve nature, notwithstanding its abun-
dant capabilities.

Wil-

William Fitzofborne, led the Norman van, at the battle of Haftings. He was created earl of Shrewfbury; had vaft poffeffions in Pembroke and Cardigan fhires, and a grant from William the Conqueror, of whatever he could win from the Welfh in Powis.

We met our horfes at Llechryd bridge, a little below which, are fome large and expenfive works, lately erected by a company, for the purpofe of making tin plates.

From thefe works the beauty of the river diminifhes, but we were

in-

informed, that at fome diftance upwards, the Tyvy is ftill more picu-
refque.

However, here we left it, and followed our coafting road, through a
miferable country, that would fcarcely bear any other inclofure than earth
and turf.   All the high lands, are fo
expofed to the weftern ftorms from
the Irifh fea, that vegetation is check-
ed by them, and even the hardy
plants of thorn and elder, are here
never feen without blafted tops.

Furze fences have lately been introduced, and we faw fome of them
thrive very well on the earthen banks.
                                    I think

I think it much to the credit of
the inhabitants of this inhofpitable
coaft, that, what can be cultivated
of it, is improved, as far as art and
manure ean affift it. Small is the en-
couragement of agriculture on this
mountainous track, where the pro-
fits will fcarcely repay the labours of
the induftrious hufbandman! From
many parts of thefe hills we plainly
difcovered the high lands of Ireland.

The town of Llanarch confifts of
a few ftraggling cottages, but the
name ferved us as a guide to Aberyft-
with: for we foon found it neceffary, to be previoufly acquainted with

H 3 every

every place in our rout; as we could
feldom get any farther intelligence,
from the few people we met on the
road, than to the next town or village.   But indeed, the intricacies of
this ride were frequently relieved by
proper direction pofts.

We now left a deep and fhady dale
on the left hand, and foon after defcended to Aberayron.

From hence, the fhore becoming
more level and agreeable, the road
quickly paffes by the intrenchment of
a fmall caftle, half of which has long
fince been wafhed away by the fea.

There

There are feveral old encampments in this neighbourhood, on the mountain tops, and I forgot to notice one, which ftands about the midway between Cardigan and Aberayron; it is very large, and has a fecond circular intrenchment within it.

About two hundred yards on the left hand of the road, and two miles beyond Llanrufted, are two fuppofed Druidical fepulchral monuments; they are upright fingle ftones, and one of them, when perfect, meafured eleven feet in height above the ground, and five feet fix inches in breadth.

H 4                    Abe-

Aberyſtwyth is ſituated on an eaſy elevation, in the midſt of a broad vale, at the mouth of the river Yſt-wyth.   All the towns beginning with Aber, denote their being near the mouth of a river; for Aber, in Welſh, is a ſmaller ſtream, diſcharging itſelf into a greater, or into the ſea.

This town carries on an inconſi-derable trade, at preſent; for the bar of the haven is ſeldom practicable for large veſſels, excepting in ſpring tides.   The herring-fiſhery flouriſhed here about thirty years ſince, but that fiſh is now a ſtranger to the coaſt.

There

There is a feafon, in the warm months, for bathing at Aberyftwyth, and the beach, which has an eafy and regular fandy declivity, is very fuitable for that purpofe.

Part of the old wall of the town is remaining, but all the facing ftones have been taken away. The caftle has undergone the fame fate, and the ruins of it are now trifling, except one, a Gothic tower, the fhell of which remains for a fea mark.

According to Powel, Gilbert Strongbow built a caftle on this

fpot,

spot, so early as the year 1107,
to secure his newly acquired possessions, which was destroyed and
levelled to the ground in 1142.
We learn, from the same historian,
that the present castle was founded
by king Edward I. in 1277, a few
years before his complete conquest of
Wales.

A regular modern ravelin is advanced before the gateway, which
was perhaps thrown up in the time
of the protectorship, at which time,
the castle was garrisoned by Crom-
well's soldiers.

The

The fpurious fepulchre of the bard
Talieffin, who flourifhed in the fixth
century, and which ftood near the
highway, about four miles from
Aberyftwyth, has, within thefe five
years, been entirely plundered, and
the broken ftones are now converted
to gate-pofts.

It is certainly much to be lamented, that the antiquities in thefe and
fome other parts of the principality
are not better preferved. How can
the inhabitants be fo negligent of
ther real interefts! and why will
they deftroy the almoft only induce-

ment

ment for ftrangers to vifit this miferable coaft ?*

From Tal y bont, our late long
*tædium* began to find fome relief
from a chearful fylvan fcene, which
conducted us by the fides of two
waterfalls, near Gwellyn-gwin bridge,
to the banks of the Dovy.

The profpect before us is now enchanting ; while the ftriking con-

* This rage for the deftruction of Pagan remains, is attributed by fome to the zeal of the
modern Methodifts who abound in thefe parts.
Perhaps this conjecture, ridiculous as it at firft appears, may not be totally without foundation. For
to what abfurd and contemptible lengths has not
fanaticifm been carried in all ages !

traft

tract of the prefent object, to the melancholy wafte we have lately left, makes us more fenfible of the pleafing tranfition.

The navigable Dovy runs through a broad expanfe of rich meadows, encircled with a majeftic chain of fuperb mountains, the flopes of which are beautifully chequered with corn-fields, paftures, and large woods.

A fmall land flood prevented my crofling the Dovy at this fpot, where there is a confiderable iron-work, to Penhal ; for which reafon, I follow-

ed

ed the rocky and picturefque road
to Machynlleth.

I was here informed, that the old
church at Penhal, which was partly
built with the ruins of the adjoining
Roman fortrefs of Kevan Caer, had
been taken down about fix years, and
that a new church had been erected
with the materials. The prefent
church is wholly covered with a
ftucco, by which the Roman bricks
are concealed from view.

Machynlleth lies in a fmall ver-
dant plain, furrounded with mountains. It ftands in the extreme weft
angle

angle of Montgomeryſhire, and the bridge from the town carried us into Merioneth.

I cannot omit a <u>ridiculous</u> cir- *too ridiculous to be mentioned* cumſtance, which occured to us at the inn of Machynlleth.

A gentleman of the neighbourhood politely introduced himſelf to us, and hearing we travelled to ſatisfy our curioſity, civilly offered to gratify it, as far as he could. It was natural for me, among other things, to enquire about the roads, and the inns: I therefore aſked him, if there were a good houſe at our

next

next ftage ? He anfwered, there were many, Mr. Lloyd's, Mr. Powell's, Mr. Edwards's, &c. I ftill enquired which was the beft : he replied, they were all very good : but to make him explicit, I perfifted in afking him, whether either of them was as proper, as that in which we were? " Sir !" faid he, with a peevifh furprize, " fhould you take this houfe for a Gentleman's ?"

I quickly explained myfelf, and begged his pardon. We might indeed have travelled through the whole country with a conftant fuite of recommendations; and this gentleman

tleman preffed us to accept of his to
his hofpitable friends; ' but it did not
agree with our plan, nor had we re-
folution enough to facrifice our time
to a daily fucceffion of jolly company.

Leaving Machynlleth we foon
found ourfelves in a truly alpine valley; the rapid torrent, roaring over
a bed of broken rocks, and now and
then interrupted by immenfe fragments, from which it fell inconfider-
able cataraĉts; the woody and exalted
precipices on each fide of the river,
and the mountain brooks continually
rattling about us, formed a miniature
piĉture of the romantic road between

I                    Aigues

Aigues belles and mount Cenis. Towards the extremity of this beautiful
scene, the huge mountain of Cader
Idris presented its naked, craggy and
prominent cliff, full to our front :
I never saw an object more awfully
sublime ; it extends more than half a
mile in length, and is at leaft a thou-
fand feet high.

The road paffes under part of this
gloomy and tremendous precipice,
on the right hand, within fight of a
large lake on the left, and clofe to
the brink of a fmaller.* It then

crofses

* This fmall lake, which is counted bottomlefs,
is called the Pool of the Three Grains, from three
im-

crofles an arm of Cader Idris, and with a quick defcent of two rocky miles, ends at Dolgelley. Part of this latter path leads through a thin oak wood, which hangs over an impetuous torrent, foaming down a rug-ged declivity, as fteep as the road.

immenfe ftones lying near it, by the fide of the road. The common people affured us, with great gravity, that thefe were only three grains of gravel which the giant Idris finding uneafy in his fhoes, fhook out at this pafs, where he ftopped to drink. I mention this ridiculous ftory, as it ferves to fhew the extravagant ideas which the Welfh ftill entertain of the fize of their ancient giants; for each ftone is larger than moft of their houfes. Upon better information I was told this water had been founded, and that it is in reality about fixty fathoms deep. The three large rocks near it, are undoubtedly fragments of the impending mountain detached from it, many immenfe crags of which appear at prefent ready to fall on the head of the paffenger.

I 2                    The

The wretched town of Dolgelley is finely fituated upon the Avon's bank: the vallies around are richly inter-fperfed with woods and decent houfes, while the mountains bound every profpect from the town, at irregular diftances.

Cader Idris, from the quicknefs of its afcent and the nearnefs of its fum-mit, appears much higher than it really is; many people, on this ac-count, have confidered it as the higheft mountain in Wales, but Snowden is indifputably higher.

I could learn no intelligence of its real perpendicular elevation: but I

fhould

should think, it must be more than half a mile above the level of the river at Dolgelley, which receives the tide at a small distance below the town.

There appears some spirit in the flannel trade in this neighbourhood, which extends its busy influence for many miles round the country.

We now passed near the poor remains of Vennar Abbey, or Kinner, according to Speed, and crossing the river Mothvaye, soon traversed another alpine vale.

I 3

About

About five miles from Dolgelly, (a few large Scotch firs, on each fide of the road, marking the fpot) we turned upwards on our left, to fee a waterfall behind a fmall houfe of a widow Vaughan. This cataract is broken into two broad parts; the upper defcends about thirty-five feet, upon a fmall craggy ridge, and the lower about twenty feet, into a romantic bafon, encircled with perpendicular or impending rocks: a fine wood furrounds it, and fome of the largeft trees project their fhady branches over the precipices of the cafcade.

Returning

Returning to the high road, we foon croffed a bridge, under which the torrent rattled from the above cafcade, down a fteep declivity, and through large disjointed fragments, towards the river.

We quitted the valley two miles farther, and afcended a barren and difmal mountain : the road continued lonefome and melancholy for feveral miles, but at length conducted us to a comfortable little inn, at Tan y Bwlch.

My companion's curiofity, led him to turn to the right hand from nearly

I 4      the

the summit of the mountain, which is called Pen maen, towards the falls of the rivers Mothvaye and Cayne. He found the road exceedingly bad, but his troublesome ride was amply repaid by the objects in pursuit; the cataracts were very deep, and fell in broad sheets of water, through a varied scenery of woods and rocks.*

* These remarkable cataracts, are each of them the fall of a whole river, and situated within a quarter of a mile of one another. That of the Mothvaye forms two very broad sheets of water, divided about half way down by a ridge in the rock, each part being also beautifully broken by frequent crags projecting through it: this whole fall may be about seventy or eighty feet in depth.

That of the Cayne is a continued steep fall from rock to rock, not near so wide as the former, but

These

These waterfalls are near a farm house, called, according to the English pronunciation, Tydunglādus, which lies in one of the roads from Dolgelley to Tan y Bwlch ; but if we had followed that rout, we must have neglected seeing the other cascade behind Mrs. Vaughan's house, the name of which is Dol y myllyn.

In an excursion, from Tan y Bwlch towards Harlech, we deviated a lit-

much higher : I should imagine it must be from 150 to 200 feet high, but the bottom is of very difficult access. The scenery, which immediately surrounds them both, is noble beyond description, producing a fine contrast to the naked hills in their neighbourhood.

tle

tle from the road, to fee the Rhaidr
du, or black cataract; fo called from
the colour of its water.

This is a fall of the rivulet Velen-
ryd, about forty feet in depth: regular bafon, femicircled with rock,
and furrounded with a thin grove,
receives it.   The reft of the valley is
poor and uninclofed.‡

As we approached Harlech, the
road became fcarcely practicable;  it

‡ The river, firft rufhes foaming down a fteep channel in the rock, for the length of about 300 feet before it comes to the precipice, over which it falls in a
large fingle fheet, into a beautiful bafon. The bottom of this cataract is alfo of very difficult, if not
dangerous, accefs.

was

was literally a ftair-cafe path, worn on the fide of a fteep precipice of a craggy and disjointed mountain.

We had as yet feen no caftle fo perfect as this at Harlech; the fhell is entire. I have no doubt, but that the prefent fortrefs was erected by Edward the Firft: the embattled turrets, the Gothic and nearly horizontal windows, the terrace, which furrounds it, and the whole form of the building, declare it to be of that age. It is fituated on a very high rock, projecting in the Irifh fea, the deep foffe on the eaft or inland fide of it, has been formerly excavated, and

worked

worked to a perpendicular, with immenfe labour ; for, on this fide only,
it feemed pregnable.   There are a few
flying arches over the gateway, which
are circular.

When we reflect on the natural
ftrength of this caftle, and the almoft
impaffable mountainous roads which
lead to it, we muft be aftonifhed
at the rafhnefs of an earl of Pembroke, who dared attempt the fiege
of it, for Edward the Fourth, in the
year 1468. We muft be ftill more fur-
prifed when we learn, that it was foon
furrendered to his attacks, though
they were carried on without the af-
fiftance

fiftance of gunpowder; for the military ufe of that murderous combuftible was ftill undifcovered, though the compofition was not unknown.

This earl of Pembroke, the year following, was defeated at Banbury, by the earl of Warwick and duke of Clarence, and after being beheaded by them, was buried in Tintern abbey.

Sir John Wynne, in his hiftory of the Gwedir family, quotes the following Britifh lines, on the ravages that were committed by him, through the counties of Merioneth and Denbigh.

Har-

Hardlech a Dinbech pob dor
  Yn Cunnev,
Nanconway yn farwor,
  Mil a phedwarcant mae Jor
A thrugain ag wyth rhagor.

" At Hardlech and Denbigh every house was in flames, and Nanconway in cinders; one thousand and four hundred from our Lord, and sixty and eight more."

In order to avoid the goat track of our morning ride, we returned over the sands of the Traeth Bychan, which are paſſable only at low water.

It is remarkable, that we had hitherto never deviated from the true line

line of our rout, when alone: and that we feldom failed of doing it, when we employed a guide.

Our prefent Cicerone from Tan y Bwlch, conducted us wrong both to and from Harlech; and on our return we were obliged to have guide upon guide, before we ventured to crofs the fands, which are by no means difficult when known, but which, from their fhifting and quicknefs, are intricate and dangerous to ftrangers.

A Welfh guide blunders through his rout, and left his knowledge

fhould

fhould be fufpected, will make no enquiry about it, till he himfelf is really
alarmed; and then he becomes more
terrified, than thofe he pretends to
conduct.

This was the precife fituation of our
Harlech attendant, for we could not
perfuade him to advance a fingle ftep
before us, either over the fands or
through the waters of the Traeth
Bychan, which is an arm of the fea,
of confiderable breadth, even at the
loweft ebb.

This was the fourth guide which
we had engaged: the firft was from
Caer-

Caerphyli to the Pont y Prîdd, for which we had no occafion, if we had taken the moft agreeable road: he happened to be very intelligent.

I took another from St. David's to the Maen figl, for which too there was no occafion, as the thing itfelf was not worth feeing. But, though the diftance was not more than two miles from St. David's, yet the guide could not find the ftone, till he had left me within 200 yards of it, and enquired at a diftant cottage after it.

The third voluntarily offered to attend my companion from St. Da-

K                              vid's

vid's to Fisgard, and this last lost the right track in such a manner, that I, though alone, arrived at Fisgard half an hour before him, notwithstanding the Maen sigl led me three miles about.

The sepulchre near Harlech, mentioned by Gibson, is still called Coeton Artur, and by the description of the country people, remains in *statu quo*.

The other monuments near Michneint mountain, are much injured by time and violence. I did not attempt to see them, on account of the difficulty

ficulty of the road from Feftiniogg, from which they are diftant about three miles. I was informed at this laft wretched town, that a Mr. Vaughan had lately dug up the ground under one of them, but that he could not difcover the fmalleft veftiges of any human interment. They might perhaps have been erected in memorial only of a battle on that fpot, the tradition of which is ftill current.

We were induced, by the cleanlinefs of our little inn, and the attentive complacency of the landlady, to fleep three nights at Tan y Bwlch.

K 2 This

This is a single house, in the parish of Feſtiniogg, and about three miles below it: the river Dryryd divides the inn from the parish church of Maynturogg; it lies in a deep and narrow valley, between the mountains, which are but moderately cloathed with wood, excepting near the houſe, where the ſylvan walks, amid the craggy precipices, are extremely picturesque.*

* This place would afford a charming retreat for a painter, delighting in romantic nature, as its environs abound with ſcenes, every way picturesque. Woody hills, naked mountains, rocky rivers, foaming cataracts, tranſparent lakes, ruined caſtles, catch the eye on every ſide of this ſequeſtered ſpot, which ſeems to want nothing, but fine weather and a ſerene ſky, to afford as rich ſtudies as the neighbourhood of Tivoli or Freſcati.

At

At a little diftance from the inn, on a woody mountain's fide, is a pleafant feat of a widow Griffith; and here, I cannot but confirm the remark of the author of the Letters from Snowdon, that the women in this country generally furvive the men, who commonly fall an early facrifice to intemperance. A heavy glutinous ale has charms enough to debauch the fenfes of the whole principality. In our journey, we frequently found the moft retired ale-houfes filled with the middling gentry, who count it unbecoming their character to retire fober. " The poor, through neceffity, reap the benefit of

K 3　　　　　　　their

their climate, and live to advanced
ages, while the richer heir feldom
waits long for the poffeffion of his
eftate, and feldom long enjoys it."
Sir John Wynne, who wrote about
the year 1600, complains againft this
vicious cuftom of his countrymen,
and fpeaking of an ancient feftival,
fays, that " my anceftors fpent the
day in fhooting, wreftling, throwing
the fledge, and other acts of activity,
and drinking very moderately withal,
not according to the *healthing* and
gluttonous manner of our days."

We now traverfed a defolate and
cloud - capt country ; but as it
hap-

happened to be low water, we avoided some of these mournful mountains, by descending on the sands of the Traeth Mawr, which carried us to the Pont Aberglaslyn, which divides Merioneth from Caernarvonshire.

This bridge is one wide stone arch, and is built over a roaring water-fall, from two perpendicular precipices. ‡

Here

‡ The author of the letters from Snowdon, seems to have confounded Pont Aberglaslyn, with another remarkable arch, called the Devil's bridge, which is thrown over a deep glen, between Aberystwith and Llanidlos in Montgomeryshire, but of which we had no intelligence, till since our return. According to our information, this bridge connects

K 4

two

*He is all confusion ℺*

Here we paufed—the grandeur of
of the fcene before us, impreffed a
filent admiration on our fenfes.—
We at length moved flowly onward,
contemplating the wonderful chafm.
An impending craggy cliff, at leaft
800 feet high, projects from every
part of its broken front ftupendous
rocks of the moft capricious forms,
and fhadows a broad and tranflucid
torrent, which rages like a cataract,

two lofty precipices, and being lately in a very ru-
inous ftate, the county thought proper to rebuild
it. The difficulty of ftriking a centre over fuch a
depth, muft occur to every one, and therefore the
architect prudently formed a centre upon the old
arch, on which the prefent bridge was built. The
timber frame being removed, the two archeſs, one
under the other, make a very fingular appearance.

amid

amid the huge ruins fallen from the mountain.

The disjointed fragments of the oppofite declivity, crufhing their mouldring props, feem fcarcely prevented from overwhelming the narrow ridge, which forms the road upon the brink of the flood.

The romantic imagination of Salvator Rofa, was never fired with a more tremendous idea, nor has his extravagant pencil ever produced a bolder precipice.

Leaving with regret this fublime and unparralled pafs, which continues

nues for near a mile, we purfued
our rout through the miferable town
of Bethkelert, over a rocky defert
at the foot of Snowdon, and by the
edge of two lakes, one of which com-
mands attention from its fize and the
fcenery around it, to Llyngwennyn
bridge, near which is a picturefque
water-fall.

A vale begins now to open, which
gradually fpreads itfelf into the pleafant and rich country around Caernarvon.

The ftreets of Caernarvon are
neat and clean. The prefent town
was

was founded in a peninsula on the
the Anglesey strait, by Edward I.
who fortified it with a wall and castle, on the complete conquest of
Wales.

The shell of the castle is entire,
and is a fine object, being faced with
a bright and durable stone; I could
not learn from whence this beautiful
stone was brought; but it certainly
came from a distance, as the houses
of Caernarvon are built with a coarse
rag stone, or brick. Every part of
the castle is Gothic, and the walls of
it and of the town, still retain their
original whiteness.

Strangers

Strangers are fhewn the tower, famous for the birth of the firft Englifh Prince of Wales, Edward II. but furely the birth of fuch a degenerate and daftardly tyrant reflects little honour on the caftle of Caernarvon.

A broad and pleafant terrace furrounds the walls of the town, which formerly contributed much to the ftrength of it, as the outward wall of the platform had an embattled parapet towards the water.

A turnpike road, to which we had been long ftrangers, carried us within almoft a conftant view of the county

county and ftrait of Anglefey, to the city of Bangor, a fmall town, with fome decent houfes in it.

We might have left Bangor a mile on our right hand, by following a nearer road, which would have conveyed us directly to the ferry, which croffes into Anglefey.

As I had, in a journey from Ireland, traverfed this ifland, and fcarcely found any thing worthy attention in it, excepting Druidical remains, which had nothing either certain or wonderful in them, we took the direct road from the ftarving inn at Porthatheu to Beaumaris

I fuf-

I fufpect that many of our Druid antiquaries, are by far too fanguine in their favourite purfuit, and that they attribute to religious ufes, what was originally intended only for private advantage.

A profufion of learning has been expended upon the Carneds of Wales, when I am convinced many of thofe heaps of ftone were piled together, for no other reafon than that the reft of the field might afford a clearer pafture.

In the melancholy wafte between Pont Aberglaflyn and Llyngwennyn,
I ob-

I obferved many *modern* Carneds, which had been thrown up in large piles by the induftrious inhabitants, for that profitable purpofe.

I pafs no reflection on the fingle monuments, or on the circular up-right ftones, which abound in moft parts of this country. Thefe may perhaps deferve notice; but a ftranger would fcarcely make them the principal object of his tour, as they will not bear a comparifon with Stone-henge or Abury, either in magnitude of ftones, or regularity of defign.

Beaumaris ftands in the pleafanteft part of the ifland, and is a handfome town.

town. The castle which was built by Edward I. is so entire, as to give a perfect idea of the plans and uses of the fortresses of that age : and even the little chapel on the west side of the quadrangle, and the adjoining oratories connected with it, are in singular preservation. The castle is flanked on all sides with a strong wall, and round towers at regular distances, the interval between it and the outer wall being about fifty feet wide. All the arches which support any weight, as in the gateways, doors, &c. are Gothic.

We may naturally conclude, that the Gothic architects thought no form

of

of arches fo ftrong as their own ; for in the caftles founded by Edward I. we fee none circular, excepting a few flying arches; which, detached from the walls, and fpringing from the towers of the gateways are advanced before the parapet, and ferved only to protect the befieged on the parapet, in cafe the gate fhould be affailed.

This is the principal diftinction between the Norman buildings in South Wales, and the Gothic in North Wales; In the firft, the cir-cular arches fupport the heavy parts, and in the laft, they fupport nothing.

L                    I en-

I entirely agree with Mr. Barring-
ton, that the plans of the Welsh
castles, founded by Edward the
First, were borrowed from the
Asiatick fortresses which that prince
had seen in the Holy Land, because
they are precisely similar to many
which Le Brun hath copied and in-
serted in his valuable travels.

But that the pointed arch derived
its origin from that country, as some
have pretended to prove, I can by no
means assent to; for nothing of that
kind appears throughout all Syria,
in any of the Saracen buildings; nor
even in the christian, except in the
ruins

ruins of the two churches at Rama and Akari, both which were founded by the European croifaders.

Others maintain that this ftyle of architecture was brought into Spain by the African Moors; but in the Moorifh remains in that country, as I have been well informed, the arches are always circular. The cathedrals of Burgos and Toledo are indeed Gothic; but it is well known, that thofe fabricks were erected in the reign of Ferdinand the Third; the firft in the year 1222, and the laft about the year 1240.

It

It is much eafier to deftroy an hy-
pothefis, than to fupport one : but,
for my own part, I fee no reafon
why this mode of building might
not have originated in the northern
parts of Europe, as probably as in
either Afia or Africa.   And does not
the term *Gothic*, which is univerfally
adopted by all the modern languages,
and applied to this particular ftyle,
feem to confirm my conjecture ?

Moreover, I may add, that the
old writers were of this opinion, and
have uniformly attributed the pointed
arch to the Goths ; and among others,
Vafari, in his account of architecture,

ture, has the following obfervation
on it: " *Queſta maniera fu trovata
da i Gothi, che per aver ruinate le
fabriche antiche et morti gli architetti
per le guerre, fecero dopo chi rimaſe
le fabriche di queſta maniera ; le quali
girarono le volte con quarti acuti, et
riempiereno tutta Italia di queſta ma-
ledizzione di fabriche.*"

" This method of building was
invented by the Goths, who, having
deſtroyed both the ancient edifices
and the architects, during their cruel
invaſions, conſtructed the preſent fabricks, in the faſhion which they now
appear in. They turned their arches

L 3                                    to

to a fharp and pointed angle, and
filled all Italy with this prepofte,
rous and unnatural mode of archi,
ture."

We croffed the Menai ferry at
Beaumaris, and a four miles ride over
the fands at low water, where the
true path was fufficiently pointed out
by pofts at proper diftances,* carried
us to the Irifh turnpike at Llanāber
in Caernarvonfhire,

* Thefe fands however are fo extremely level,
that they are in a manner inftantaneoufly over-
flown when the flood comes in ; travellers therefore
who intend croffing them, fhould make exact en,-
quiries concerning the tides, an inattention to
which has been fatal to many.

At

At the foot of Penmaen Mawr ſtands a ſmall inn, the landlord of which is a ſenſible and ingenious ſurveyor.

It was under his inſpection, that this famous road has been lately made perfectly good, and as ſecure as poſſible. It is broad and excellent, and is cut along the ſide of a cliff, (which it divides in two parts) impending over the Iriſh ſea, and is guarded with a wall.

But it is not in the power of human art to remove all danger from this tremendous paſs. For large frag-

ments,

ments, frequently falling from the upper precipice, fometimes interrupt the road, and fometimes are impetuoufly driven through the parapet into the fea.  I faw many inftances of thefe horrible fractures, which had been recently made.

I was informed by the landlord, that he had lately attended an Englifh gentleman, to the fummits of Penmaen Mawr, and of Snowdon, in order to take their elevation. The perpendicular height of the firft is 1400 feet, and of the latter, fomething about 1300 yards above the fea level.

It

It may appear extraordinary, that I have as yet taken no notice of the mountains of Plinlimmon or Snowdon; when it muſt have been ſeen, that I was at the feet of both:—but in truth, the atmoſphere was ſo conſtantly obſcured, whether from the nature of the mountainous country, or from the general cloudineſs of the ſeaſon, that their upper parts were always hidden from our view.

We had a glimpſe, for a few minutes only, of the ſummit of Cader Iris from Dolgelly.

During

During our abode amid thofe fuperb mountains, neither fun nor ftars
appeared to our fight for feveral days ;
and, wrapt up in an impenetrable
mift, we were perpetually enveloped
with a twilight obfcurity. Our fituation was like a fcene of enchantment,
impreffing a fuperftitious extafy on
our fenfes, while we contemplated
the fublime operations of nature
around us.

But on our emerging from thefe
romantic vifions, the firft view of the
chearful rays of the long abfent fun,
gave an inexpreffible refrefhment to
our fpirits—it faluted our immediate

ap-

approach to the vale of Caernarvon,
We changed the climate in an in-
ftant—we breathed a freer air.

Here I fenfibly felt the force of an
expreffion in the whimfical life of
Benvenuto Cellini, which directly
occurred to my memory. He had
been long imprifoned, in a dark fubterraneous dungeon, in the caftle of
St. Angelo at Rome. He bore with
fortitude his miferable deftiny, and
would have been even eafy with it, if
a fingle beam of light had been per-
mitted to enter his melancholy den :
in vain he prayed for a momentary
view of the fun ; his cruel guard de-
nied

nied him that common privilege. At
length a dream reprefents the glori-
ous luminary to his fight, when, in
a tranfport he exclaims—O brilliant
orb! whom I have fo long ardently
languifhed to behold! Henceforth let
me gaze on thy brightnefs for ever,
though blindnefs be the confequence!

The fituation of Conway is exceedingly fine: it lies on the bank of
a noble river, and in the centre of a
beautifnl vale, well cultivated and
woody.

Here we found a confiderable al-
teration in the manners of the people.

We

We were now in the great Irish
road; the article of eating was dou-
bled in our bills, and the door of our
inn was crouded with beggars.

I don't recollect to have seen one
beggar before in the whole tour; the
common people were indeed poor
enough, but they seemed contented
with their lot, and were always
willing to answer our enquiries, without the least expectation of any re-
ward: they never asked for it, and
when we sometimes gave the half-
cloathed wretches a shilling, they re-
ceived it with an aukward surprise,
and were so confounded, that they

could

could only exprefs their thanks in tears of gratitude.

The town of Conway is fmall, and indifferently built ; it was fortified with walls, which ftill remain, and a caftle, by Edward the Firft.

The plan of the caftle is eafily traced ; it ftands on a rock clofe to the river ; the ruins are very large, but the moft remarkable room in it, is the great hall,   which is 129 feet in length, and 31 feet 4 inches in breadth; the height was 22 feet from the floor to the point of the Gothic vault, fix ftone arches of which are ftill perfect.

fect. There are three chimnies in it.
The form of this hall is irregular,
and appeared to me to be three
fides of a decagon. It was conftructed
in this manner, becaufe the fhape of
the rock would not admit of fo much
fpace in a right line.

On the fouth fide of the caftle, the
towers are partly founded on the
rock, and partly on the fteep declivity of it, and one of them remains a
very fingular ruin: the lower part
has flidden down the precipice fome
years fince, and lies in large fragments on the fands beneath, while
the upper part of the tower continues

nues perfect, and projects at leaft
20 feet beyond the walls below.

It appears, at firft fight, wonderful
how it can continue a moment in its
prefent impending pofition ; but it is
thus preferved, by the firmnefs of
its cement, and the ftrength of the
inward foundation.

As Chefter fair was now approach-
ing, the inns of Conway were filled
with linen merchants from Ireland ;
and as there were not beds for the
whole company, a party of them,
not unwillingly, facrificed the night
to Bacchus, in the adjoining room

to

to my chamber: the melody of a
blind harper, accompanied with the
Welſh ſongs of the maid of the inn,
encouraged the libation; which, to
my agreeable ſurpriſe, was unattend-
ed with either riot or noiſe. This
was the only harp I heard in the principality, both the inſtrument and
voice were perfectly pleaſing, and the
muſic being truly Welſh, was plain-
tive and melancholy. I thought my
ſituation ſo happy, that I did not lament the interruption of my ſlum-
bers, or wiſh the harmonic ſociety at
a greater diſtance.

M        I made

I made a diligent enquiry through all Caernarvonſhire for the Glyder mountain, which Gibſon has particularly deſcribed, and which, from its ſingularity, I much more wiſhed to have ſeen, than the ſummits of either Plinlimmon or Snowdon: theſe a conſtant hazy atmoſphere forbade us even to attempt. I could, however, learn no certain intelligence about it, neither from the name, nor from the deſcription of it.

On the utmoſt top of this mountain, according to the continuator of Camden, who ſaw it, is a prodigious pile of ſtones, many of which are

are of the magnitude of those at Stonehenge. They lie in such an irregular manner, crossing and supporting each other, that some people have imagined them to be the remains of a vast building; but Gibson more naturally supposes them to be the skeleton or ruins of the mountain; the weaker parts of which may have been worn away in a series of ages, by the rains and meltings of the snow.

On the west side of the same mountain, he speaks of a remarkable precipice, adorned with numerous equidistant columns, formed to that shape

M 2 by

by the almoſt continual rains, which
this high rock, being expoſed to the
weſterly ſea wind, is ſubject to.

Notwithſtanding the ſituation of
this mountain ſeems to be pointed
out by the laſt line, and though its
phænomena are ſo peculiar, yet we
were obliged to leave the country,
without gaining the ſmalleſt knowledge of it.

We croſſed the wide ferry at Conway, which brought us into Den-
bighſhire, and traverſed a hilly country, till we came within eight miles
of

of St. Afaph, when we entered the fertile vale of Clwyd.

We paffed over Penmaen Rofs in this morning's ride, where the declivity is fteep and the road ‖indifferent: a nearer path is cut, for horfes, along the fide of the fea cliff, in the fame manner as at Penmaen Mawr, but it is fo formidably narrow and unprotected, that few people dare truft themfelves or their horfes on it.

The city of St. Afaph, in Flintfhire, is a neat and pleafant village, fituated on an elevated bank of the

M 3 Clwyd:

Clwyd: the cathedral has nothing to recommend it, but a proper cleanliness.

An excurfion carried us to the large and well built town of Holywell, fo called from the famous spring of St. Winifred.

This fpring is fo ftrong, that it actually flows at leaft a ton of water in a minute, which has been experimentally proved. But the whole legend of the faint is a mere modern invention; for Giraldus, who never neglected an opportunity of celebrating Welfh miracles, is entirely filent on this head, though he lodged one

night

night at Bafingwerk, within a mile of Holywell.

The countefs of Richmond, mo-ther of king Henry the Seventh, founded the elegant little cloyfter which covers the well; and over it a chapel, which is now ufed as a public fchool.*

M 4                    In

* The well is ftill in fome eftimation, particu-larly among the catholics, for the falubrity of its fpring; and not without reafon, if we may credit the numerous trophies of hand-barrows, crutches, &c. which adorn the roof; and which have been left at different times by pious patients, whofe faith contributed undoubtedly not a little, towards making them whole.

The

In our return, we ſtopt to ſee Rydland Caſtle, a ſmall ſquare fortreſs of
Norman architecture, in which there

The waters are made uſe of internally and exter-
nally, and both at the ſame time; ſo that according to the Author of the Bath Guide,

   " While little Tabby is waſhing her rump,
   " The ladies are drinking out of the pump."

As this baſon is open to all comers promiſcuouſly,
the ceremony of ablution ſeems to be performed,
by both ſexes, without much regard to delicacy;
a thin linen ſhirt being the only covering made uſe
of by either. While we were here, we were entertained with the ſight of a fine ruſtic Venus, emerging from the tranſlucid waves, whoſe cloſe-clinging
wet drapery ſhewed her firm and athletic limbs, to
ſuch advantage, that we could not avoid telling her,
we preſumed ſhe bathed merely for pleaſure; but
ſhe aſſured us, notwithſtanding appearances were ſo
*ſtrongly* in her favour, that ſhe came there for a
violent rheumatiſm, for which ſhe had found great
relief. It is certainly a fine cold-bath.

is

is no appearance of any Gothic ad-
dition. It was rebuilt by Henry the
Second; and Giraldus, in his itinerary, was nobly entertained in it,
foon after it was finifhed.

This caftle is noted in hiftory, for
the famous ftatute enacted in it by
Edward the Firft, in the year 1284,
for the better government of his
newly acquired dominion; and the
preamble of this ftatute informs us
of the entire fubjection of Wales.

Leaving the Irifh road at St.
Afaph, we foon arrived at the picturefque town of Denbigh, which

is built on the declivity of a lofty
hill, on the higheſt point of which
are the ruins of a ſtrong caſtle of
the time of Edward the firſt. The
principal gateway is a beautiful Gothic arch, and the king's ſtatue remains in a niche over it, in the ſame
manner as at the caſtle of Caernarvon.
The original town ſtood upon
this hill, and the walls of it are ſtill
viſible, but at preſent the pariſh
church only remains on it, near which
is the unfiniſhed ſhell of a larger
church, with a nave and two iſles,
which appears to have been begun
in the fifteenth century. It is now
a ruin.

Ruthin

Ruthin is a large and populous town on the Clwyd, it was formerly protected with a Gothic caftle, but the remains of it are very trifling.

About five miles from Ruthin we quitted the charming vale of Clwyd, which for beauty and richnefs is not excelled by any fpot of the fame magnitude in the whole ifland. It is well wooded and well inhabited, and the river runs through the whole length of it.

This delightful vale is of an oval fhape, twenty-fix miles in length and about eight wide, in its broadeft part;

it

it is wholly bounded with high hills, excepting towards the Irish sea, where it ends in a Marsh at Rydland.

Our scene was now changed to a mountainous heath, which however plentifully supplies the lower countries with coals and lead.

The descent of this hill, towards Wrexham, overlooks the extensive level of the vale royal of Cheshire. At the foot of it, we passed Offa's dyke, or the Claudh Offa, which is very visible on each side of the road: it was thrown up by order of Offa, king of the Mercians, in the eighth century,

century, as a boundary between his and the Britiſh territories. This dyke began at Baſingwerk in Flint-ſhire, and ended at Chepſtow, being a line of more than a hundred and fifty miles.

Wrexham is a handſome and well built town, ſurrounded with an in-cloſed and fertile country. The church is large, and was erected in the reign of Henry the Seventh. The tower is 140 feet high, and is beautiful ſpecimen of the florid or reformed Gothic, which taſte began to prevail about the time of that king, when the windows were made

broader

broader and lefs pointed at the top, ·
their arches being more rounded at
their fprings, and ending with an
obtufer angle.

I have called this the reformed
Gothic, not on account of its being
a better ftyle, but becaufe it was a
variation from the then eftablifhed
model.

Within the church is an ancient
ftone monument of a man at full
length, with his legs extended, and
a fword parallel with them, the hilt
of which is in the right hand ; on
the left hand is a fhield with a lion

or

or wolf rampant, and round it are some large Saxon characters, which would be legible, if the monument were placed in a proper light; but at prefent it lies under the gallery ftaircafe, whither it was brought, about forty years fince, from the walls of the church yard.

We left a large new built feat of Sir Watkin Wynne's on our left hand near Ruābon, and foon after found ourfelves on the banks of the Dee, between the mountains.

Llangollen is a miferable town, but romantically fituated in a fmall

dale

dale closely. environed with mountains, which are finely varied with woods, rocks and torrents. On the point of one of them, just above the town, are the ruins of the castle Dinas Brân, but the badness of the weather prevented my inspecting them.

The river Dee is a noble object, as seen from the bridge at Llangollen, it rages furiously down the broad, shelving, solid rock, which is worn to a kind of glossy polish by the run of the water, and which forms the bed of the river for a considerable space.

On

On our arrival at the inn at Llan-gollen, we found it in the poffeffion of fome mourners, who were juft re-turned from the funeral of a friend; however fome tolerable quarters re-mained for us.

The difmal folemnity of thefe weeping countenances foon evapo-rated, and the forrows and fenfes of the company were quickly drowned in large potations of ale. Such is the general conclufion of a Welfh meeting, whether it be merry or melancholy.

I was here informed, that a burial was efteemed the moft profitable

N

function

function of a Welſh clergyman.
The neighbours and relations of the
deceaſed attend in large numbers at
the funeral, and make conſiderable
offerings to the officiating prieſt; for
they are taught to believe that their
reſpeſt to their friend's memory, is
in proportion to the oblations they
give.

Though the man who was here in-
terred was but a common tradeſman,
yet the collection at the church
amounted to more than five pounds.

This cuſtom is evidently derived
from the ancient maſs money collected

for

for purgatory indulgences, and it is fortunate for the clergy of Wales, whose income is generally moderate, that the superstition has suffered no reformation.

We now ascended the long narrow ridge of a mountain, which soon brought us within sight of Chirk castle.

The ancient outward walls and towers of this castle still remain, but the court or quadrangle has at different times been made habitable; the apartments range all around it, and the principal suite of rooms are

N 2   grand

grand, and handsomely fitted up in the modern fashion.

Chirk castle was founded by Roger Mortimer in the thirteenth century, who usurped large possessions in this country from his Welsh ward. It stands on a lofty eminence, commanding a rich and extensive view over part of the counties of Cheshire and Shropshire, and nearly in the centre of a park, which the proprietor, Mr. Middleton, is now levelling and forming to the present taste.

From hence a melancholy ride over a lonesome, mountainous heath,

at

at length brought us into the vale of Llanrhaidr. We were advised to take a guide through this tedious road, and the caution was not unnecessary, for otherwise we should have been in a continual uncertainty, without a possibility of enquiring for a step of the way.

From Llanrhaidr we rode along the bank of the river on the north side for nearly five miles, to see the noble cataract, called, by way of eminence, Pistill Rhaidr; for Rhaidr means a cataract, and the river is so called on account of the rapidity of its torrent, and Pistill signifies a water-spout.

N 3                    On

On our approach towards it, neither the fize of the river, nor the
firft view of the fall, which we faw
at the diftance of two miles, gave us
any idea anfwerable to our expecta-
tions; but as we advanced, a noble
theatre of naked perpendicular rock,
opened its grand femicircle to our
fight: in the middle of it fell the
Piftill Rhaidr, in a large body of
water, from the amazing height of
two hundred and forty feet.

This cataract may be divided into
three parts: the firft fall defcends
about one hundred and fixty feet,
upon a ridge in the precipice; the

water

water next breaks through a large
natural arch of the rock, over which
a man might walk, though not without difficulty and danger, and foams
into a fmall bafon about twenty-five
feet lower ; it then rages through an
horizontal chafm, and falling forms
the river below.

There is another confiderable cafcade of the river within a few yards
of the bottom of the rock, which, in
any other place, from the water-wear
of the rocky fragments and the magnitude of them, would claim its proper attention.

A little

A little below, ſtands a craggy in-
ſulated column, cloſe to the river's
brink, which the frequent inunda-
tions from the Piſtill Rhaidr have
worn to that pictureſque figure, by
waſhing away the ſurrounding mould.
Mr. Brydone, or the Canonico Re-
cupero, might poſſibly determine, in
how many thouſand years the rock
could acquire its preſent elevation. *

* It is a compliment juſtly due to the vicar of
Llanrhaidr, Dr. Worthington, to mention that,
under his patronage and influence, a ſmall building
has been erected near this famous caſcade, for the
convenience and ſhelter of travellers in this preca-
rious climate, and that a new and nearer road is
carrying on from the town to the Piſtill, the old
one being exceeding bad. The roads indeed in
general, within the circle of this gentleman's
neighbourhood, bear the marks of an active and
public ſpirited magiſtrate.

Llan-

Llanvyllyn is a neat and decent town, fitnated in a pleafant valley of Montgomeryfhire. From hence, by an indifferent road, through another valley, and over the deep river Vurnwy, we arrived at Welfh Poole, a large, populous, and well built town, at a fmall diftance from the Severn.

This famous river is navigable to the quay of Welfh Poole, which is about two miles from the town, and which is at leaft 200 miles from its mouth at the Briftol channel.

Powis Caftle ftands about a mile above the town, the gardens are laid out

out in expenfive parallel terraces, hanging over each other, in the tafte introduced by king William, and bordered with fantaftic yews, and other formal ever-greens.

The caftle is ftill inhabited, but has more the appearance of a long-neglected manfion, than that of a comfortable houfe.

Both the gardens and buildings are in fuch a mournful decay, that we thought our time ill fpent in vifiting them. The profpect from the caftle is extenfive and fine, over a broad and rich vale.

We

We were told at Welſh Poole, that the preſent lord intended to re-form the whole, and indeed we ſaw ſome preparations for that purpoſe, as a large quantity of unpacked boxes of furniture, and a long narrow gallery in the firſt court, refitting for a ball-room.

We croſſed the Severn about two miles from Welſh Poole, over a long narrow bridge, and ſoon reached the neat little town of Montgomery.

On our approach to it, the town, and the caſtle above, ſituated on a high rock, the ſide of which, to-wards the town, is thinly chequered

with

with trees, prefented a very picturefque view.

There is but one fign of an arch
in the whole ruin, it is of a win-
dow, and appeared to me, from the
remaining fprings of it, to have been
Gothic.

On a mountain ftill above the caftle, and overlooking it, is a large
double intrenchment ; I obferved another on this fide of Llanvyllyn, and
another S. W. from Welfh Poole.

Leaving Montgomery, we foon
defcended into a beautiful valley, diverfified

verfified with the Severn meadows
and paftures, and bounded, on each
fide of the river, with moderate hills,
generally mantled with wood.

There are no remains of the caftles
of Delevorn and Caerfufe, in the
vicinity of Newtown; the intrenchment of the firft appeared to us, from
the oppofite fide of the Severn, in
our road through the valley.

Materials for building being rare
in this country, the neglected caftles
were foon effectually plundered for
private ufes. The houfes are here
generally framed with timber, and
the

the intermediate parts are fenced from the weather with laths and plaister.

Newtown is built in this manner, which, in other respects, is a neat town, agreeably situated on the Severn's bank, at the extremity of the valley before described.

Four miles carried us to the summit of a mountain, the ascent to which begins at Newtown; the path over this mountain is intricate and boggy, but we were fortunate enough to find it, though the disagreeable uncertainty of being in the right track,

preyed

preyed upon our spirits for many miles.—We afterwards dipt into two or three Radnorshire dales, and arrived at Llandrindod.

We had many views of old intrenchments from this rout, but they afforded a small relief to the *tædium* of crawling through vile roads, and a melancholy waste.

While we were paffing over the mountain, the path was suddenly interrupted by a wide bog, but we thought ourselves happy in seeing an old woman, of whom we might enquire the road, riding along the

oppo-

oppofite edge of it. We called to her, we holla'd, but in vain; for, whether fhe was totally deaf, or whether fhe was afraid for her purfe or her chaftity, fhe flogged her poney into a canter, without even deigning to turn her face towards us.

Thus left in a ridiculous predicament, and commenting on the novel drollery of the fcene, we ventured, after a confiderable paufe, to lead our horfes through the bog, which happily we found founder than we expected.

The

· The wells of Llandrindod are fitu-ated in a wild extenfive heath, fome fpots of which are rarely enlivened with a few trees, and fmall cultivated inclofures. The mountains bound the dreary profpeÆ at a diftance.

The lodging houfe is tolerably contrived for the reception of com-pany, and in a fine fummer, is fre-quently full. Notwithftanding the badnefs of the weather, and of all the roads in the environs, we found a decent fociety at Llandrindod, both of gentlemen and ladies, but they were chiefly invalids. Our party at dinner and fupper, for we all

O                              ate

ate together, was from fifteen to twenty.

We croffed the Wye at Builth, which brought us into Brecknock-fhire.

Builth is a fmall town, fituated in a broad and pleafant plain; it was in this neighbourhood that prince Llewelyn was flain in a wood, after a defperate conteft between the Britifh and Englifh forces, at a bridge upon the river Yrvon, wherein the former at length were entirely routed.

We paffed through Builth on a market day, and our ride through the

the crouds in the ftreet was attended
with fome difficulty. It at firft
amazed us, to fee the fullnefs of
thefe weekly meetings in fuch little towns, as they appeared more
like large fairs than common markets; the houfes were not fufficient
to contain the people who thronged
to them, nor the ftables their horfes.
We could fcarcely conceive, from the
general wildnefs of the country,
that it could have poffibly produced
fuch numerous affemblies; but as the
towns in Wales are rare, the markets
are attended from villages and ham-
lets, at confiderable diftances, for no
fhops are to be found in the parifhes,

O 2                          nor

nor are the fmalleft trifles to be pur-
chafed, except in the towns.

The chief pride and glory of thefe
little communities, arife from the fullnefs of their markets, and the num-
ber of their annual fairs : thefe laft,
collect the country people in fuch
quantities together, that the traveller
through Wales ought to be conftantly upon his guard againft them, or
otherwife, he might find himfelf
greatly diftreffed for want of lodging and accommodations.

From Builth we rode over another
long, lonefome, and boggy mountain,

tain, from which we defcended into a pleafant valley, and good turnpike road, about five miles from Brecknock.

Brecknock is a large handfome town, fituated on a fine rifing above the Ufke. The Monuchdenny or Pennervaen, as it is commonly called, is a very high mountain on the fouth fide of the town, and from the quicknefs of its afcent, bears fome kind of miniature refemblance to Cader Idris, above Dolgelly, in Merionethfhire.

A few walls, and fome remnants of Ely tower, on the keep of Breck-

O 3

nock

nock caftle, are ftill vifible. The walks behind the great church, on the hill, are exceedingly pleafing, and though acceffible to the public, are laid out with tafte, and preferved very neat; they are formed on the fhady declivity of the hill, the foot of which is wafhed by the torrent of the river Honthy. The remains of the old college are near the Ufke, and part of them, as well within the prefent chapel as without, are as old as the original foundation, which was laid in the reign of Henry the Firft.

Several

Several old encampments are to be feen on the hills about Brecknock; but the moft remarkable fortification is y Gaer, about two miles N. W. from the town,—This laft is indif-putably Roman, and is fituated on a gentle eminence, at the conflux of the rivers Efkir and Ufke. Part of the walls is ftill remaining, which are exactly fimilar to thofe at Caer-leon. I was fhewn a fquare Roman brick with LEG. II. AVG. finely im-printed on it, which was dug up at this camp.

The turnpike now follows the current of the Ufke, being commonly

O 4

within

within view of it, through a delicious vale, which is diverfified with
paftures, woods and mountains ; the
lands are wholly cultivated to the
beft advantage, and are well inhabited.

Near the five mile ftone from
Brecknock, the pillar noticed by Gib-
fon, ftands upright on the road fide,
but *Victorini* is the only legible word
on it. We faw the ruins of Tre-
tower caftle on our left hand, and
the remains of Crickhowel, clofe to
the road on our right ; the keep of
the laft will foon be the only veftiges
of the caftle, as the materials are

now

now daily carried away for private purpofes.

The environs of Abergavenny in Monmouthfhire, are rich and beauti-ful, and like the reft of the vale from Brecknock, abound with the moft charming variety of landfcape. The profpects are terminated at proper diftances with mountains, among which, at the oppofite fides of the town, Skirid vawr and Blorench raife their confpicuous heads.

The town has a few good houfes fcattered in it, but in general the ftreets are narrow, ill paved and ill built

built. Some of the walls and part
of the tower on the keep, are the only remains of a once flourishing Norman caftle. My curiofity did not
lead me to vifit the new college or
feminary, which was lately founded
in this neighbourhood, by the *pious*
munificence of a right honourable
lady.

This academy is inftituted for the
inftruction and maintenance of fuch
youths who may fhew any froward
or extraordinary fparks of genius.
The ftudents may be taken from
the cottage or from the field, without diftinction of rank or age, but
their

their abilities or their *call* muft be indifputable, before they can be admitted within the facred walls ; thefe are the only qualifications.    The *elect* are here taught the grand *art* of regeneration,  and in due  time are to be fent forth as apoftles, to impofe their dangerous fuperftition on the weak minds of the credulous multitude.*

* Going, about three years ago, out of curiofity into a celebrated methodift chapel at Bath, I recollected, in the perfon of the preacher, a man who had lived in a family of my intimate acquaintance in the capacity of coachman, and on enquiry was informed, that he had ftudied and taken his degrees in this new founded college, from whence he had juft emerged, to undertake the guiding of fouls inftead of horfes.

In

In confequence of the following elegant defcription of Llantony abbey, by Giraldus Cambrenfis, I could not refift the temptation of making an excurfion to the ruins.

*Stat in valle de Ewyas profundiſſima, quantum ſagittæ eſt arcu jaƐtus emiſſæ, montibus ethereis orbiculariter undique conclufa, ecclefia Joannis Baptiſtæ plumbeis laminis coperta, lapideo tabulatu pro loci natura non indecenter conſtruƐta. Vere religioni locus idoneus et diſciplinæ canonicæ præ cunƐtis inſulæ Britannicæ cœnobiis competentiſſimus, a duobus eremitis in honorem eremiticæ vitæ primo fundatus, ab omni*

populari

*populari ſtrepitu in ſolitudine quadam longe remotus, ſuper fluvium Hodeni per vallis ima labentis ſitus.*

*Hic clauſtrales in clauſtro ſedentes cùm reſpirandi gratia forte ſuſpiciunt, ad quaſcunque partes trans alta teĉtorum culmina, montium vertices quaſi cœlum tangentes, ipſaſque plerumque feras (quarum hic copia eſt) in ſummo paſcentes, tanquam in ultimo viſas horizonte proſpiciunt. Hora vero diei quaſi inter primam et tertiam ſuper montium cacumina vix emergens et ſereno tempore corpus hic ſolare primo conſpicitur."*

"In

" In the deep vale of Ewyas, which is not more than a bowſhot wide, ſtands, encircled with an amphitheatre of immenſe mountains, the church of St. John ; it is covered with lead, and not inelegantly built, with an arched roof of ſtone. This ſpot is juſtly ſuited for religious exerciſes, and the moſt proper for canonical diſcipline of any other monaſtery in the Britiſh iſland.

" The church was firſt founded, ſolitary and remote from all worldly noiſe, by two hermits, to the honour of a monaſtic life, and is ſituated on the river Hodney, which runs through the length of the vale.

" The

" The cloistered monks may view, from within their walls, the mountains rising above them and almost touching heaven with their exalted summits, and abounding with deer feeding aloft, at the extremity of the lofty horizon.

" The sun is never visible to this gloomy recefs, till between the afternoon hours of one and three; and even then, is rarely feen, except in the cleareft feafon."

In my ride to this romantic abbey, I left the high Hereford road near the five mile ftone, and turning

to

to the left, followed the fource of
the murmuring Hodney for an hour
and a half, and then croffed the river, juft under the ruins.

The foregoing picture from Giraldus is mafterly drawn, and though
touched with a poetical pencil, is very
accurate.   The church is really encircled with mountains, for the open-
ing through them to the vale is not
vifible from the cloyfter.

The monks indeed were not fo
very much deprived of the chearful
rays of the fun, for *that luminary*
fhone upon the ruins, at the time
I faw them, at eleven o'clock.

The

The lower parts of the mountains, and the valley itfelf, are enriched with meadows and corn fields, and are now and then enlivened with a little wood.

The abbey church was built in the form of a crofs, and is ftill a noble object; it was founded, according to Speed, in the year 1137, and is a regular compofition of Norman architecture, mixed with Gothic. I call it regular, becaufe all the underftructure is Gothic, and the upper Norman, the arches below being all pointed, and thofe above circular; and becaufe it was built upon one en-

P                                     tire

tire plan, and manifeftly at one and the fame time.

The whole nave, the roof excepted, remains, from eaft to weft; and is, by my meafurement, two hundred and twelve feet in length, and twenty-feven feet four inches in breadth; the ifles are no more than eight feet eight inches broad. The ftone diagonal vault over the body of the church, fprang from fmall cluftered flying pillars; thefe are ftill feen projecting from the walls, between the Gothic arches of the nave.

Two

Two fides of the high tower are ftill extant, which rife from nearly the centre of the church.

The whole ftructure is faced with a durable and well worked ftone, and the ruins offer as romantic a view as any in the tour.

Juft above the little parifh of Llandewi, four miles below Llantony, is a remarkable mountain, the fides of which have, at different times, been broken from it, and now lie in immenfe fragments underneath, having left a long perpendicular precipice more than 100 feet high.

I could

I could learn no particulars about these separations of the rock, though from the apparent freshness of some of the fallen pieces, I do not conceive the last to be very ancient.

Several stupendous fissures and chasms appear on and about the mountain of Skirid vawr, the foot of which I passed in my morning's ride. These were occasioned by the same cause as the separation of the rock near Llandewi, which in all probability proceeded from its foundation being weakened or destroyed, by the frequent burstings of the springs below; when the sinking or

division

divifion of part of the rock would
naturally follow, from its great impending weight.

But the inhabitants of Abergavenny attribute the rents of Skirid
vawr to another caufe; and wifhed
me to believe that they were the mi-
raculous effects of the convulfions
of nature, on the day of the cruci-
fixion.

The country ftill continues to wear
the fame rich drefs as about Abergavenny, even to Monmouth, with the
difference only, that it is now more

P 3                    enlarged,

enlarged, and unconfined with mountains.

Ragland caftle, which lies partly
in the road, is a magnificent ruin ;
the magnitude of it, and the large
remains, are uncommonly ftriking.

It is greatly to the honour of the
duke of Beaufort, the proprietor of
this caftle, that he has endeavoured
to preferve from deftruction all the
remains of religious and military architecture of which he is the pof-
feffor.

Tin-

Tintern abbey, Chepftow and Ragland caftles, all in this county, are
inftances of his laudable veneration
for antiquity, which defervedly ex-
cites the gratitude of every curious
traveller, who muft often lament, in
his Welfh tour, that the noble exam-
ple is too rarely imitated.

Ragland caftle is of no great age;
the foundation was begun in the reign
of Henry the Seventh; parts have
been added at different times; the windows of the great hall are in the tafte
of Elizabeth's reign, and feveral of
the ftone chimney-pieces are ftill of
a later date; fome of thefe remain

un-

uninjured in the walls above the buttery (according to the college phrafe) and are ornamented with a light regular frieze and cornice, that would not be confidered as inelegant, even at prefent.

Camden calls Ragland, a fair houfe of the earl of Worcefter's, built caftle-like.

The extenfive outworks were added by the marquis of Worcefter, in the civil wars, and he fortified them in fuch a manner, that he was enabled to hold Ragland for king Charles, till his imprifonment at Holmby.

This

This castle had the honour of being the last which surrendered to the all-powerful forces of the Parliament.

Monmouth is a large and handsome town, and well inhabited by gentry: but I may say of the castle, which even flourished in the time of William the Conqueror, and has been since famed for giving birth to our English hero, Henry the Fifth,——*etiam periere ruinæ.*

I crossed the Wye at Monmouth, and traversing the forest of Deane in Gloucestershire, finished my tour

at

at Beachly; where the ferry boat, with a ftrong wind, wafted me over the Servern to Auft, within ten minutes.

ROUT

# R O U T

## O F   T H E

# T   O   U   R.

| | Miles. | | Miles. |
|---|---|---|---|
| From Auſt to | | *Brought over* | 55 |
| Beachly | 2 | * Caerdiff | 13 |
| * Chepſtow | 3 | Llandaff | 2½ |
| Persfield | 2 | Cowbridge | 10½ |
| Tintern | 4 | * The Pile | 12 |
| * Chepſtow | 6 | Margam | 3 |
| Caldecot | 5 | Aberavon | 4 |
| Caerwent | 2 | Briton Ferry | 3 |
| Caerleon | 9 | * Swanſea | 5 |
| * Newport | 3 | Llandebēa | 17 |
| Machen | 6 | * Llandīlo vawr | 5 |
| Bedways bridge | 4 | To and from | |
| * Caerphyli | 2 | Caſtle Caraig- | |
| Pont y Prîdd | 7 | cennin | 9 |
| | 55 | | 139 |

| | Miles. | | Miles. |
|---|---|---|---|
| *Brought over* | 139 | *Brought over* | 333 |
| * Caermarthen | 15 | * Machynlleth | 6 |
| St. Clare - - | 9 | * Dolgelly - | 16 |
| Narberth - - | 13 | Dôl y myllyn | 5 |
| ** Haverford- | | *Tan y Bwlch | 15 |
| weft - - | 10 | Rhaidr du - | 3 |
| Harbarfton - | 10 | Harlech - - | 10 |
| To and from | | ***Tan y Bwlch | 9 |
| Pembroke - | 16 | PontAberglaflyn | 7 |
| *Haverfordweft | 10 | Bethkelert - | 1 |
| Solvath - - | 12 | Bettus - - | 8 |
| * St. David's - | 4 | * Caernarvon - | 5 |
| Y Maen figl - | 2 | Bangor - - | 9 |
| Fifgard - - | 18 | The Ferry - | 1½ |
| Newport - - | 7 | * Beaumaris - | 5¼ |
| Nevern - - | 2 | Llanaber - | 5 |
| * Cardigan - | 10 | * Conway - - | 9 |
| Llechryd bridge | 4 | Abergele - - | 11 |
| Llanarch - | 18 | * St. Afaph - | 7 |
| *Aberayron - | 4 | Holywell - - | 12 |
| Llanrufted - | 9 | Rydland - - | 12 |
| * Aberyftwyth - | 9 | *St. Afaph - | 3 |
| Tal y bont - | 7 | Denbigh - - | 6 |
| Gwellyn gwin | 5 | * Ruthin - - | 8 |
| | 333 | | 507 |

| | Miles. | | Miles. |
|---|---|---|---|
| *Brought over* | 507 | *Brought over* | 607 |
| Wrexham - | 16 | Llandwy - - | 5 |
| Ruābon - - | 5 | Llanbadern vawr | 3 |
| * Llangollen - | 6 | ** Llandrindod | 4 |
| Chirk Caftle - | 5 | Builth - - - | 7 |
| * Llanrhaidr - | 14 | * Brecknock - | 15 |
| To and from | | Crick howel - | 13 |
| Piftill Rhaidr - | 9 | ** Abergavenny | 6 |
| Llanvyllyn - | 5 | To and from | |
| * Welfh Poole | 12 | Llantōny - | 24 |
| Montgomery - | 8 | Ragland - - | 9 |
| * Newtown - | 9 | * Monmouth - | 8 |
| Llanbādern vy- | | Beachly - - | 16 |
| nydd - - | 11 | | |
| | 607 | TOTAL - | 717 |

We lay at the places marked with an afterifk, and if any place is marked with more than one, we ftaid fo many nights at it as there are afterifks.

The diftances were generally regulated by the watch, and therefore they may be fometimes a little more, and fometimes a little lefs, than meafured miles.

*F I N I S.*